Pete Seeger's Storytelling Book

OTHER BOOKS BY PETE SEEGER

Where Have All the Flowers Gone

Everybody Says Freedom (WITH BOB REISER)

Abiyoyo

Carry It On! (WITH BOB REISER)

The Foolish Frog (WITH CHARLES LOUIS SEEGER)

Henscratches and Flyspecks

The Incompleat Folksinger
(EDITED BY JO METCALF SCHWARTZ)

Hard Hitting Songs for Hard-Hit People
(WITH ALAN LOMAX AND WOODY GUTHRIE)

The Twelve-String Guitar as Played by Leadbelly
(WITH JULIUS LESTER)

The Bells of Rhymney and Other Songs and Stories

American Favorite Ballads

The Steel Drums of Kim Loy Wong

How to Make and Play a Chalil

The Caroler's Songbag (WITH THE WEAVERS)

How to Play the Five-String Banjo

Pete Seeger's Storytelling Book

PETE SEEGER

and

PAUL DuBOIS JACOBS

Harcourt, Inc.

New York   San Diego   London

Requests for permission to make copies of any part of the work should be mailed to the following address: Permissions Department, Harcourt, Inc., 6277 Sea Harbor Drive, Orlando, Florida 32887-6777.

www.harcourt.com

Library of Congress Cataloging-in-Publication Data
Seeger, Pete, 1919–
Pete Seeger's storytelling book/by Pete Seeger & Paul DuBois Jacobs.
p.   cm.
ISBN 0-15-100370-X
1. Storytelling. 2. Tales.   I. Jacobs, Paul DuBois.   II. Title.
GR72.3 .S44 2000
808.5'43—dc21   00-029599

Designed by Susan Shankin
Text set in Berkeley Book
Printed in the United States of America
First edition
J   I   H   G   F   E   D   C   B   A
Permissions acknowledgments appear on pages 263–4, which constitute a continuation of the copyright page.

For Danny, Mika, and Tinya

Contents

PREFACE

This book could never have been written by me alone. At age eighty and busier than ever, I knew I needed help. Fortunately, I came across a young and well-organized writer, Paul DuBois Jacobs, grandson of an old friend of mine. We got down to business: me tape-recording stories, Paul rewriting them, then both of us reworking each other's drafts. Along the way, we tried the stories out on family, friends, parents, and children. Now, thanks to editors, papermakers, printers, truckers, salespeople, and all the other folks who get books into people's hands, we try them out on you. Here's hoping these stories leave you with a few new favorites and some ideas to tinker with.

Pete Seeger

ACKNOWLEDGMENTS

Thanks to all the family, friends, and listeners
who helped make this book a reality.

Thanks to the Robert Francis Trust

Thanks also to Michelle Brook
and all the hardworking folks at Harcourt.

We are especially grateful for the care and
thoughtfulness of our amazing editor, Diane D'Andrade.

Love and praise to the superwomen in our lives:
Toshi Seeger and Jennifer Swender. We'd be at
a loss without their wisdom and contributions to this book.

P.S. & P.D.J.

Pete Seeger's Storytelling Book

Introduction

WHEN I WAS A small child, my father, just home from work, would come into my bedroom and tell me stories of family adventures and fantastical foolishness. Lying there in the dark, I'd whoop with excitement. He'd say to himself, "I'm supposed to be putting this child to bed. He's more awake than ever." But, exhausted by laughter, I'd soon fall sound asleep.

Twenty-five years later, I found myself putting my own children to bed. Back then, we lived in a small cabin with no electricity. So, like parents since the beginning of time, I started telling stories in the dark. And although I'm not the best storyteller, my children—and now grandchildren—still prefer these improvisations to reading something out of a book.

I love to draw and I love picture books. And we all know how strongly children (and adults) are attracted to television, videos, and computers—machines that present moving images right in front of their eyes. But instead of always relying on somebody else to make up the pictures, why not let the imagination take over? Let children learn what fun it is to imagine the pictures. Or give it a try yourself. See if I'm not right.

Of course, you don't have to wait until bedtime to tell stories. You may be on a long car trip or waiting at the dentist's office. Or maybe you're preparing your child for a new experience like the first day of school. And naturally, you don't have to be a parent or grandparent. You may be a teacher faced with naptime, or a summer camp counselor with a cabin full of restless kids and a rainy day. Or maybe you're a visiting aunt, uncle, or babysitter who simply wants to strike a bond.

As a young man, I didn't think of myself as a storyteller. Then, at age twenty, I met Woody Guthrie, a balladeer from Oklahoma. Soon after that, I met Lee Hays, son of an Arkansas preacher. Both Woody and Lee were great storytellers, and I listened to them with admiration.

I learned early that it's easiest to begin with something familiar. If you remember a favorite picture book, you can tell the highlights, the bare plot. You don't have to tell it word for word. Or pick something from a collection of folktales, the Bible, or even Shakespeare. Lately, I find myself telling about events and figures from American history: George Washington, for instance, or Martin Luther King, Jr., or Rosa Parks. And don't forget about your own family's history.

Sometimes you'll have thirty minutes, sometimes only two. Luckily, successful storytelling doesn't depend on a story's length. A quick personal anecdote can capture a child's attention as easily as a long tale. You might use an example from your own childhood. At eighty years of age, I still remember an embarrassing story from when I was six. My parents gave me a dime and sent me down the block to buy something that cost a nickel. I don't recall what the item was, but I met a neighbor's kid at the store, and with the extra five cents we bought a candy bar.

When I got back home, my father asked, "Peter, where is the change?"

"It c-cost . . . t-ten . . . c-cents," I said, my voice wobbling.

"Peter, you know you don't have to lie to us," my father said. He got down on his knees so that he was eye level. "What happened to the other nickel?"

Now I was bawling. "I g-got some candy," I gasped through the tears.

"That's perfectly all right," my father said. "You know we love you. You don't ever have to lie to us." He said that over and over.

I'm sure stories like this are common to all of us: stories of hilarity, terror, adventure, embarrassment. And since they're etched into our memories, they are easy to retell. What's important is to create an atmosphere of sharing.

Not long ago I thought every good story needed a beginning, a middle, and an end. Then my grandson Kitama came along. He loves to make up stories and all the names and situations that go with them. But he finds it hard to finish. One day I asked him, "Kitama, do you ever finish your stories?" "No," he answered. "I just start them."

This makes Kitama a certain kind of storyteller, and for different kinds of stories, there are different kinds of tellers. That leaves room for all of us—for you, for me, for anybody. And while it's true that some storytellers might be better than others, and some may be truly great, what a sad world this would be if the only storytellers were professionals, and the only stories were the best ones.

I think you'll discover that the more stories you tell, the more confidence you'll gain. The first book I wrote was called *How to Play the Five-String Banjo*. On page 18 it said, for the "secret of a clear crisp tone, see page 30." On page 30

it said, "Practice." It's the same with storytelling, though un-
like musicians who can practice in private, storytellers have
to practice right in front of their audience. And the more
you practice, the better you'll get at what I call "growling
them out." If it's a scary tale maybe you snarl and hold your
fingers out like claws. If it's a funny tale you might puff up
your cheeks and let out a funny noise.

Don't be afraid to embellish stories, to make up names
and places, or to add new characters and subplots. You'll be
surprised how fanciful you can get and still keep your listener's attention. Trees can talk to each other. Stars can talk
to each other. My old friend, the poet Walter Lowenfels,
wrote a book of children's stories called *Be Polite to the Grass*.
In it, every piece of furniture, every pot and pan, even pictures on the walls, take on different characters.

Try it yourself. Start with the question "What would
happen *if*...?" Then take off on any fanciful flight and follow it through to an illogical conclusion. The ingredients for
stories are found everywhere: under rocks, perched on oak
leaves, rusting behind old radiators. But don't overdo it.
Pick just one or two ideas at a time, add seasonings, and
savor them.

Now some of you might be thinking, this is easy for Pete Seeger to say. He's a professional. And true, for sixty years I've earned a living singing songs and telling stories to audiences around the world. But as Iona and Peter Opie, editors of the *Oxford Dictionary of Nursery Rhymes,* point out, "Four and twenty trained singers caroling in harmony are not so effective as one parent's voice, however out of tune."

More and more, it seems we're becoming a nation of spectators. On Sundays we watch professional athletes instead of playing ourselves; on weeknights we watch professional jesters instead of tickling ourselves; and on weekdays we tune the radio to professional music makers instead of singing ourselves. But perhaps it's wisest to view performers as intermediaries who show how enjoyable these things can be.

The world can be full of people with enough carpentry skills to make a table. Or enough sewing skills to piece a quilt. Or vocal skills to sing in a choir. Or gardening skills to grow some vegetables or flowers.

Just because we have cars and buses shouldn't mean we forget how to walk. And just because we have books and television sets shouldn't mean we forget how to tell stories. They needn't be virtuoso stories. And you don't have to look far. Tell about your family, your friends. Tell about the nation's history or a people's history. Tell a moral tale or a silly one. Tell stories even if they're only the bare plot.

My hope is that each of us, at some point in our lives, will say, "Hold on. I know that someone can do it better, but I want to try this myself. It looks like fun."

I Stories from My Father

*O*NE WAY TO BEGIN telling stories is to tell a story from your own experience. Perhaps it's a story about how Mama met Papa or the time Grandma won a brand-new car. Or perhaps it's a story full of real danger and suspense about rescuing a cousin from a lake or putting out a fire. And since these stories are from personal memory, you shouldn't have much trouble recalling them over and over again.

My father, Charles Seeger, was the first storyteller in my life, and the first story he ever told me I call "The Trailer and the Flood." It was a true story about a family trip. There wasn't much plot to the tale, but the plot wasn't important. I wanted to hear my father's voice and hear again and again how the family survived a crisis.

The story took place in 1920 when I was just a baby and my father was an unemployed professor of music. He had what he thought was a grand idea: to take classical music out to the small towns and villages of America. He wanted to introduce the beauty of Bach and Brahms to country audiences. My mother would play her violin and my father would accompany her on a little folding pump organ. That was his plan, at least.

My father spent a year meticulously building a house trailer that would serve as both home and stage. It was

pulled behind a Model T Ford, and if you've ever seen a picture of a Model T, you know what a tiny machine it was. An
extra low gear had to be put in so the car could haul the
trailer up hills. The trailer itself looked more like a fancy
covered wagon. It had four solid tires and a long drawbar
that attached to the trailer hitch on the Model T. The body
was made out of tongue-and-groove maple boards fastened
on with brass screws. The roof was made of canvas and held
up by hoops. My cradle was hung between two of the
hoops, while my two older brothers, ages six and seven, had
small bunks. At the other end was my parents' bed.

The trailer was also outfitted with a small two-burner
gas stove, a tiny icebox, and a six-by-six-foot "porch" that
could be pulled out and held up by two jacks. This served
as a makeshift stage for my parents when they performed
their music.

Of course, the whole idea turned out to be a financial
failure. A few months into the trip, my parents had to give
up in North Carolina, and the trailer eventually ended up
back in my grandparents' barn. It was hardly ever used
again.

But something positive did come of the trip: a story. It is
the first story of this book.

The second story my father ever told me, "The Foolish

Frog," was inspired by a song he remembered from his childhood. When I discovered my father could make up new stories, I demanded a new one every night. I called them "Nutty Stories." One was about an unruly pea patch, another about talking telephone lines.

Years later, I asked my father how he made up these tales. "Well," he said, "I start with an imaginary situation and see where it leads. Along the way an idea arises for how to end it." This was my first lesson in storytelling.

Many of my father's stories explored the idea that identical things might not be as identical as we think. We assume all telephone wires are the same, but how do we know for sure? We assume all oatmeal pots are the same, but how do we know for sure? In my father's stories, not even identical hair combs could be assumed to be truly identical.

The settings, props, and characters of these stories were products of my family's rural lifestyle. You could say my father stuck to what he knew. During the summers we lived at my grandparents' country home sixty miles north of New York City. There was a hayfield and a cow pasture, and my father kept a garden. There was even a little brook. We lived in the barn and got our water in pails from the house. We didn't have electricity, but we did have a kerosene stove and lanterns in case we wanted light. Usually we just ended the day early and got up early.

In the late mornings my father would say, "Let's go see what's good to eat in the garden." Then, out in the garden, he'd say, "I wonder how this would taste with that." And we'd make combinations that had never been made before. We cooked Swiss chard with beets, or onions with green beans. Each summer brought new adventures. One year it was hiking; another year it was building model ships; another year it was model airplanes. They were special times that, not surprisingly, found their way into my father's stories.

By the time my own children came along, I could only recollect a handful of the dozens of stories my father must have told me during those years.

Here they are.

THE TRAILER AND THE FLOOD

LONG AGO BEFORE radio and CD players were in every home, a music professor said to his violinist wife, "I've had enough of playing for rich city people. Why don't we take our beautiful music out to small-town and country audiences?"

So they piled their three small sons into an old Model T Ford, hitched up a homemade trailer, and set off for the countryside. Back then, a ride in the country was a bumpy one. Roads were not paved as they are today; most were full of ruts and stones. The trailer bounced around on its solid rubber tires, up and down, side to side.

Then one day it began to rain. . . .

And rain.

Cars of long ago didn't have side windows made of glass

like cars do today. When it started raining, all the young family could do was put up a piece of canvas with a panel of what was called "isinglass." Through this, they could see outside dimly. And what they saw were puddles. Puddles everywhere. As it kept raining, the puddles got bigger and bigger, deeper and deeper, until the entire road seemed like one big puddle.

"Don't you think we should stop somewhere?" asked Mother.

"Better to get to a town," said Father. "There must be one just a few miles down the road."

And they kept on going. Slowly.

The surrounding countryside was flat. Fields stretched out on either side of the road. After a while, so much rain had fallen that the road and fields were completely underwater. Mother was getting nervous. "Charlie," she said, "we should stop or turn around."

"I can't turn around on this one-lane road," said Father. "But if it will make you happy, I'll get out and check anyway." The road was really narrow, and in order to turn around, Father saw that he would have to disconnect the trailer and leave it behind. "Nope," he said, climbing back into the Model T. "It's impossible to turn around. We better keep going before this water rises any farther."

"But how will you know if we're on the road?" asked Mother. "I can't even see it."

"See the fence posts on each side?" said Father. "As long as I stay halfway between the fence posts, I know I'm on the road."

His answer certainly didn't calm Mother. Sheep were sloshing through the fields, no longer able to graze. The rain came down so heavy and so fast that all the family could see was rain, rain, rain. They couldn't see trees. They couldn't see houses.

"Charlie," said Mother, "please turn around. The hubcaps are almost underwater."

"That's all right," said Father. "The water can go over the hubcaps as long as it doesn't reach the carburetor." And the little Model T just kept chugging away.

"Charlie, we're going to be drowned!" cried Mother. "I can carry the baby, but the boys are too big. They'll be swept away. And if you try to hold them, you might get swept away, too."

"No, it will be all right," said Father, even though he was also worried. He knew it wouldn't be safe for the family to get out of the car and try to walk. Sticks and grass were already beginning to snag in the wire fences. There could be a flash flood and everybody would be swept away.

Chug, chug, chug. Blurddddd went the Model T Ford, pushing on, pushing on. The family looked to either side of the road. There wasn't a thing to be seen. Not even cows, who must have taken refuge on high ground.

The water was getting deeper and deeper and deeper. Father knew it was foolhardy, but he drove on. "No sense stopping here," he said.

"But we can't go on like this! What happens if the water keeps on rising?" said Mother.

"It's got to let up sometime," said Father. "In fact, I think it's getting better already."

Chug, chug. Brrrrr.

And sure enough, the water was going down from a foot deep to only half a foot deep.

Chug, chug, chug. Bwrrrddrr went the Model T Ford.

Yes, it looked like . . . maybe . . . the road was rising out of the water. Miraculously, the Ford kept chugging ahead, pulling the trailer, pulling the family, until the whole lot rolled up onto firm ground, dripping like a wet cat. The family was safe!

But Mother had seen enough. "That's it," she said, "we are going back to the city."

"I'm afraid we can't go back until next spring," said Father. "The roads are in worse condition than I thought."

"Then we'll stay here," said Mother. "We're not going any farther." And that night the family camped near the little town of Pinehurst, North Carolina. They slept in the trailer by the side of the road and woke up in the morning to find a group of local farmers with guns surrounding them. Father quickly put on his clothes. "What's the matter?" he asked them.

"We don't want no gypsies around here," answered the farmers.

"We are not gypsies," said Father in his New England accent. "We are musicians."

"You're what?" the farmers said.

"Musicians. My wife is a violinist. And here's the organ I play." Father pointed inside to a little folding pump organ. "We perform in towns and villages."

The farmers looked in and saw the instruments. "Actually," said Father, "we need a place to spend the winter. Do any of you know where we might camp with our trailer?"

"Well, I've got a woodlot out behind my house if you don't mind camping in the woods," said a farmer named McKenzie.

Father gladly accepted the offer and parked the trailer in the small woodlot. He chopped down some trees and built a framework sixteen feet square. Then he put an army squad tent on top, a woodstove inside, and the family lived there through the winter. You can imagine what it was like for Mother with her violinist's fingers washing diapers in a big iron pot over an open fire.

Mother and Father ended up becoming good friends with the McKenzies. One night they took their instruments up to the McKenzies' farmhouse to show their generous hosts what kind of music they played. Mother played her violin and Father played his little folding pump organ: Bach, Brahms. The McKenzies sat there politely and said, "Oh, that's very nice. We play a little music, too." And they took their fiddles and banjos down off the wall and proceeded to fiddle up a storm.

Father said he realized then that country people had a lot of good music themselves. "They didn't need my city music as much as I'd thought."

I'm sure we all have stories like "The Trailer and the Flood": stories of family outings whose retelling over the years turns them magically into something approaching legend or tall tale. I was only a baby at the time of this story—too young to recall the

actual trip. But when I was four and my father retold the story to me, it was as real as anything. I couldn't hear it enough. Now, at age eighty, I can't remember any more of it than I've told. But my guess is that my father spun the story out for as long as he could, embellishing it here and there.

My older brother John recently told me that he'll never forget that winter in North Carolina for as long as he lives. Although he was only six at the time, he remembers digging for potatoes and carrots in bins of sand. He remembers the dirt floor of the army squad tent. He even remembers our father taking a guitar up to old Mrs. McKenzie, who was bedridden, to sing her some songs.

I often wondered if any of the McKenzies still lived in Pinehurst, North Carolina, but it took seventy-five years to find out. When I was singing in Chapel Hill in 1995, a woman came up to me after the concert. "Are you related, by any chance, to the Seeger family that had a trailer they brought to Pinehurst in 1920?"

I said, "Good Lord, are you part of the McKenzie family?"

She nodded. "My grandmother never stopped talking about that family from New York who spent the winter with them. So you're really from that same Seeger family?"

"Yes," I said. "I was the baby."

Now looking back, I realize I've spent a lifetime trying to bring the good music of country people to the ears of city people. Who knows? Maybe it was the sound of that old-time music of the McKenzie family that planted the seed of banjo picking inside me.

THE FOOLISH FROG

ONCE UPON A TIME there was a farmer walking down the road, whistling a tune to himself:

He said, "Doggone, I wish I had some words for this song. All I've got is the melody."

Just then he came to a little bridge. He leaned on the railing and looked down at the brook. There was a big old bullfrog, hopping from bank to bank, *z-z-zt, boing, z-z-zt.* The bullfrog looked up, saw the farmer, and figured he'd show off. He took an extra . . . big . . . **hop.**

Z-z-z-z-z-ztt!

He landed *splash!* in the mud and got himself all dirty. The farmer laughed and laughed and started singing:

Way down south in the Yankety Yank,

A bullfrog jumped from bank to bank,

Just because he'd nothing better for to do.

He stubbed his toe and he fell in the water,

You could hear him holler for a mile an' a quarter,

Just because he'd nothing better for to do!

Now the farmer went walking down the road feeling mighty proud of himself for making up a song. He went down to the corner store. Bought himself some groceries, a pair of work gloves, and a plug of chewing tobacco.

"Oh, before I go," he said to the storekeeper, "I have to sing you my new song."

"Go on home," said the storekeeper. "I'm busy here. See all these customers?"

"I won't pay you my money unless you let me sing my song!"

"Well, sing it then and get it over with," said the store-keeper.

The farmer started to sing and the storekeeper cried out, "Hey, that's a *wo-o-onderful* song. Gather 'round everybody, we'll have a party!" And he passed around free soda pop and free soda crackers, and the men were stamping on the floor.

Meanwhile . . .

Wives and children back at home were sitting down to supper. But where's Father?

"Children," the mothers said, "you better run down to the corner store and fetch your old man. He's probably down there wasting his time as usual."

All the children ran down the road and ran inside the corner store. Do you know, when they heard that music, they forgot all about going home. The children started singing, too:

> *Way down south in the Yankety Yank,*
> *A bullfrog jumped from bank to bank,*
> *Just because he'd nothing better for to do.*

And they were passing around the free soda pop and the free soda crackers and stamping on the floor.

Now, in every farmhouse it was the same situation.

The mothers said, "Do they expect us to work all day

and nobody show up for supper?" They started down the road, waving their frying pans. Well, as they got near the store and heard that music, they forgot about being mad. They dropped the frying pans in the gutter, walked in the store, and the mothers started singing!

> *Way down south in the Yankety Yank,*
>
> *A bullfrog jumped from bank to bank,*
>
> *Just because he'd nothing better for to do.*

And they were passing around the free soda pop and the free soda crackers, and everybody was stamping on the floor!

Meanwhile . . .

Out in the barns, all the cows started talking. "Where is everybody? We're supposed to be milked. It's getting mighty uncomfortable!" The cows left their stalls, wobbled out of the barn, down the road, and right into the corner store. The cows started singing:

> *Moo-moo, moo-moo, moo-moo-moo,*
>
> *Moo-moo, moo-moo, moo-moo-moo,*
>
> *Moo-moo, moo-moo, moo-moo, moo-moo, mooooo!*

And the cows' tails were swishing out the windows, and they were stamping on the floor and drinking the free soda pop and eating the free soda crackers.

Out in the barnyard all the chickens said, "Where is everybody? We're supposed to be fed; we're getting hungry." The chickens hopped over the fence, hopped down the road, and hopped into the store. The chickens started singing:

> *Cluck-cluck, cluck-cluck, cluck-cluck-cluck,*
>
> *Cluck-cluck, cluck-cluck, cluck-cluck-cluck,*
>
> *Cluck-cluck, cluck-cluck, cockle doodle doo!*

And the chickens were stamping on the floor, drinking the free soda pop, and eating the free soda crackers.

Meanwhile . . .

All the barns started talking to each other. "We feel mighty empty," they said, "without any cows, without any chickens. I guess we'll have to go find them." So the barns picked themselves up off their foundations, galumphed down the road, and s-q-u-e-e-z-e-d themselves into that corner store, believe it or not. Did you ever hear a squeaky hinge on a barn door? That's the way the barns sang:

Eee-ee, eee-ee, eee-eee-eee,

Eee-ee, eee-ee, eee-eee-eee,

Eee-eee, eee-eee, eee-ee, eee-ee, eeeeee!

Out in the fields, all the grass said, "Where is everybody? The cows are supposed to come and eat us. I guess we'll have to go find them." The grass picked itself up, swished off down the road, and swished right into the store. And the grass started singing:

Whsh-whsh, whsh-whsh, whsh-whsh-whsh,

Whsh-whsh, whsh-whsh, whsh-whsh-whsh,

Whsh-whsh, whsh-whsh, whsh-whsh, whsh-whsh, whshhhhh!

Of course, when the grass was gone, the fields were gone. And when the fields were gone, the banks of the brook were gone. The brook said, "I don't have any banks to flow between." The brook bubbled down the road and bubbled right into the corner store.

Bubl-bubl, bubl-bubl, bubl-bubl-bubl,

Bubl-bubl, bubl-bubl, bubl-bubl-bubl,

Bubl-bubl, bubl-bubl, bubl-bubl, bubl-bubl, bubluble!

The brook was bubbling up and down the stairway! The grass was growing out the chimney! Feathers were flying through the air! Cows' tails were swishing out the windows! Everybody was stamping on the floor, drinking the *free* soda pop, and eating the *free* soda crackers!

Meanwhile . . .

There was the bullfrog in midair.

He looked down. There was nothing underneath him! He looked over. There was no bank to land on!

"Where am I?" he asked. And he started hopping down the road, *z-z-zt, boing, z-z-zt, boing.* The road rolled itself up behind him like a roll of toilet paper.

"Hey, what's that racket down at the corner store?" said the frog. "Why, they're singing! They're singing about ME! And he was so proud he puffed himself up with pride! And he puffed . . .

and he puffed . . .

and he puffed . . .

and he—*POOM!!!*

He exploded! Cows, barns, chickens, grass, farmers, wives, children—the whole corner store went up in the air. And then everybody floated down. They landed right where they were supposed to have been the whole time. Sat down eating supper, feeling kind of foolish for themselves.

Next day they went out to find the frog. They looked high; they looked low. Soda-pop bottles and soda crackers in all directions. But no frog.

So all there is left of the frog is the song. We might as well sing 'er once again. Everybody ready?

> *Way down south in the Yankety Yank,*
> *A bullfrog jumped from bank to bank,*
> *Just because he'd nothing better for to do.*
> *He stubbed his toe and he fell in the water,*
> *You could hear him holler for a mile an' a quarter,*
> *Just because he'd nothing better for to do!*

Anybody know how to whistle? Then take 'er away.

This story is about the power of music. I liked it so much that twenty-five years after I first heard it, I told it to my own children. Years after that, somebody showed me an early ten-inch 78 rpm Victor record with music on only one side. It was from 1910, and the song was called "The Frog Song." It was sung by May Irwin, a popular comedian around the turn of the century.

There are various versions of the song in the Folksong Archives of the Library of Congress. My father just borrowed the chorus. Years later, I myself put this story on an LP record for the Folkways Company. An illustrated book came out after that, and there's even a children's video.

I retell this story now in the hope that you will make up your own version. Localize it to fit wherever you live in the world. Embellish it. Put people you know into it. Maybe you can put a very hungry person in the corner store who is just guzzling the soda pop and eating the soda crackers by the ton. Or maybe there is somebody like me who likes sweets, and they ask, "Do you have something besides crackers? How about those chocolate-chip cookies?" Perhaps instead of a corner store, it's a neighborhood market that's familiar to your child.

And don't forget to use outlandish voices to act out the singing and talking. Pretend you're a cow. Pretend you're a chicken. Pretend you're a fed-up farmer's wife with an alto voice. Pretend you're a child and use the highest voice you can manage. Pretend you're a barn door in need of oil. For the brook sound, flip your tongue in and out, fast.

My father actually made up a sequel, but neither of us could remember much of it when I finally asked him about it years later. It seemed that in the sequel, there was a terrible financial crisis and the national currency wasn't worth anything. Luckily, *the frog song became so popular it spread throughout the land and was coming out of every radio. Most people thought the song was worth more than money. They said, "Print the picture of the frog on the dollar bill, and we'll have faith in the nation's currency again." The banks said they didn't care whose picture was on the bill, as long as they had the dollar. So that's what the government did, and it brought the country out of the depression.*

That's all my father and I could remember. See if you can't make up your own sequel.

The Foolish Frog

Way down south in the Yan-ket-y Yank,— a bull-frog jumped from bank to bank— just be-cause he'd noth-ing bet-ter for to do.—

He stubbed his toe and he fell in the wa-ter; You could hear him hol-ler for a mile and a quar-ter just be-cause he'd noth-ing bet-ter for to do.—

YOP UP PEAS

EARLY ONE SPRING a father and his son were out in the garden planting peas. "Son, will you bring me a trowel?" asked the father.

"Yop," said the boy.

When the boy returned with the trowel, the father said, "Really, Johnny, you should learn to say 'yes' properly."

"Yop," said the boy.

The father laughed and shook his head, then went back to planting peas.

The next day the boy was in school when his teacher asked, "Johnny, will you bring me an eraser for the blackboard?"

"Yop," said the boy.

"Really, Johnny, you should learn how to say 'yes' properly," said the teacher.

"Yop," he replied.

The teacher sighed and shook her head.

That afternoon when the father came to pick his son up at school, the teacher mentioned to the father, "Johnny really should learn how to say 'yes' properly."

"I know," said the father. "I'll insist on it."

And all the rest of April and all during May, the father tried his best, but somehow Johnny couldn't learn to say "yes" properly. Only "yop" came out of his mouth.

His mother tried, too. She'd hear the door slam and call out, "Is that you, Johnny?"

"Yop," said the boy.

"I do wish you'd learn to say 'yes' instead of 'yop.' Won't you please try for me?" said his mother.

"Yop," said the boy.

"Oh dear, I'm afraid you'll *never* learn," said his mother. "If only I knew where you caught that bad habit. 'Yop' is a catching thing just like a bad cold."

The mother didn't know how right she was.

Back during the spring planting, the peas in the garden

had been listening to the father and son's conversation. And some of the peas had begun wondering if they could say "yop," too.

All through June they practiced yopping. No luck.

Then, early one morning in July, a ripe pea pod split open and yelled, "Yop!" And just as the mother had predicted, the yopping habit turned out to be a catching thing. It spread quickly to other peas. "Hey, this yopping is kind of fun," the peas said.

"Yop!" said one pea.

"Yop!" said another pea, until "yop!" sprung from all parts of the pea patch and woke Johnny up. Still dressed in his pajamas, he walked out to see who was in the garden.

But nobody else was out there.

"Son, is that you in the garden so early in the morning?" the father called, rubbing the sleep from his eyes.

"Yop," called the boy.

"Oh, Johnny, I don't think you'll ever learn how to say 'yes' properly," called the father.

"Yop!" said a voice nearly identical to Johnny's.

"Hey! That wasn't me. Who said that?" asked Johnny. Then a pea hit him right on the tip of his nose. "Ouch! That hurt."

The peas had done more than just picked up Johnny's bad habit! As the pods burst open to say, "Yop," the peas shot out with great force. And now they were yopping and flying everywhere as Johnny scrambled out of the garden. "Help!" he cried as he ran.

"I'm coming, son. Don't worry," called the father, using a garbage can cover as a shield. The force of the peas was so great, it made the cover ring out—*Ping! Plink! Clunk! Clink! Pang!*

"Yop!" shouted one pea.

"Yop!" shouted another, as Johnny and his father scrambled back to the safety of the house.

That night no one in the neighborhood could sleep because of the noise. By morning the peas that had sprung free were already beginning to sprout in the ground, and the sprouts were beginning to grow new shoots. You couldn't get near them! They spread like a bad cold! And these new shoots were bearing new pods which also quickly went to yopping.

The situation was out of hand. Neighbors complained. Sidewalks were blocked off. No one was safe walking within a hundred yards of Johnny's garden. Windows were broken by the sheer force of flying peas. The pea patch grew larger and larger. Within three days it turned into a huge pea thicket that spread out over the lawn, over the field, over the cow pasture.

Finally, the neighbors had had enough. They called the chief of police.

"What's that you say? An unruly pea patch? I don't believe it. I'll be right over," said the chief, who fancied himself an expert gardener as well as an expert police chief.

The chief arrived in front of Johnny's house to find the neighbors crouched behind trees and garbage cans. "What are you all hiding from? Peas? Come out this instant! You look foolish," said the chief, shaking his head. For a problem as silly as an unruly pea patch, he hadn't even turned on his siren.

"Chief! Help!" cried Johnny's father from the house.

"I'm coming, I'm coming," said the chief, hiking up his trousers. He hadn't taken more than two steps when the peas set about their yopping and zinging every which way. The chief fell to his knees and tried to lie flat (which was difficult on account of his large belly).

"Jeepers, these peas really are yopping," he said. But being the chief, he kept his wits about him and radioed the station house for backup.

Patrol cars arrived from every direction with their sirens wailing. The police were dressed in their bulletproof vests, helmets, and riot shields. A few officers arrived on farm tractors.

"Don't worry, Chief! We'll have you out of there in a second," called the sergeant over his loudspeaker.

Instead of carrying their usual equipment, the police carried sickles. Some of the police tried to eat the peas, but the chief yelled, "Quit that eating and get me out of here!"

Johnny peered out at the spectacle from the only unbroken window in the house. He was frightened.

The police lined up shoulder to shoulder, shields in front of them, and advanced on the garden, swinging their sickles. The peas yopped and flew in all directions. It wasn't long before the whole garden had been sickled and trampled into a cloud of dust and a mass of torn-up pea vines!

When the dust settled, not a single green plant was left standing. A cheer went up from the neighbors. The police were wiping their brows and catching their breath. The chief shook hands in the crowd and gave a long speech about his department's bravery, for he also considered himself an expert speech giver.

But Johnny didn't feel like cheering at all. He only felt a

deep sadness inside. The family garden was ruined. His parents were inspecting the house and property, wondering how they would fix the damage.

"Johnny, have you learned your lesson?" asked his parents severely.

And *very* quietly Johnny said, "Yes."

Meanwhile, the chief strolled across the garden battlefield and surveyed the destruction. "Well, that's the last of them," he said. "Strangest garden I ever saw." But just as he finished saying this, one last pea went "Yop!" and hit the chief right on the tip of his nose.

Language is a powerful tool as this story shows. We grown-ups often try to get children to speak what we believe is "correct" English. But let's not forget that English is a crazy language. Richard Lederer says in his great book, Crazy English, *"In what other language do people drive in a parkway and park in a driveway? . . . In what other language can your nose run and your feet smell?" Crazy.*

Sometimes while storytelling we need a word that doesn't even exist in English. So we create a word like "yop." And in this

story the repetition of "yop" invites children to actively participate in the telling. In groups of three or more, children really pick
up on this aspect and enjoy it. If they don't pick up on it themselves, give them a little encouragement. I like to hesitate before
each "yop" so they can fill it in.

Some schoolchildren have suggested replacing the sickles with
forks and knives so the police can eat the peas at the story's end.
This might not be a bad idea. After all, this world could use more
block parties. Maybe the police can get a big pot of water boiling
over a fire and they can cook peas for the whole neighborhood!
(On the coast of Maine, they might call these kinds of pots "Yop-
ster pots.") It's my belief communication is made a whole lot
easier with a little good food. And this way Johnny'd end up a
hero, even if he does get charged with "disturbing the peas."

PINK PILLS FOR PALE PEOPLE

A LITTLE GIRL was feeling pale and not too well.

Her parents said, "Oh, darling, we'll go to the doctor and see what he can do for you."

The doctor's office was filled with many other patients. Some patients had coughs. Some patients had tummy aches. Some patients had sore throats. And all of the patients were feeling pale and not too well. The little girl and her parents took their seats and waited.

And waited.

And the longer they waited, the paler the little girl felt.

Finally, a nurse called the little girl and her parents into an examining room and said, "Sorry to keep you waiting. The doctor will be with you shortly."

The doctor came in, took one look at the girl, and said, "Well, you *are* looking very pale." He took the little girl's temperature and blood pressure. He listened to her heart-beat with his stethoscope. He checked her throat using a tongue depressor.

"It seems to me," said the doctor, sounding very impor-tant, "that your daughter needs some of my pink pills for pale people. Pink pills are good for people feeling pale. You just call up the drugstore and ask for Dr. Johnson's pink pills for pale people. Your daughter will be well by morning."

When the family got home, the father telephoned the drugstore. "I need one bottle of Dr. Johnson's pink pills for pale people," said the father.

"Yes, sir, let me get you the druggist," said the clerk.

The father happened to be a musician, and while he waited on the phone, he made up a little song:

Pink pills for pale people.

Pink pills for pale people.

Pink pills, pink pills,

Pink pills for pale people.

"Yes, hello," said the druggist.

"Oh, excuse me," said the father. "I was just singing to myself. I need one bottle of Dr. Johnson's pink pills for pale people."

The druggist knew Dr. Johnson well. "Yes, sir, I know exactly which pills he's talking about. I'll have them ready right away. One bottle of pink pills for people feeling pale."

Now the telephone wire had been listening to the father sing his little song and thought it rather funny, and so repeated it to another telephone wire:

Pink pills for pale people.

Pink pills for pale people.

Pink pills, pink pills,

Pink pills for pale people.

Ha, ha, ha, ha, ha.

The next day, the mother got on the telephone to call a friend. She dialed the number. She put the phone to her ear. But before she said a word, her call was interrupted by a strange singing:

Pink pills for pale people,

Pink pills for pale people.

Ha, ha, ha, ha, ha.

The telephone wires had taught the song to other telephone wires, and those wires had taught the song to the telephone poles. And it wasn't long before all the wires and all the poles were singing this ridiculous song and having a good laugh.

That afternoon the mailman came walking along the street going from house to house to deliver the mail. And as he did, he distinctly heard high, tinkerly voices singing:

> *Pink pills for pale people,*
>
> *Pink pills for pale people.*
>
> *Ha, ha, ha, ha, ha.*

The mailman looked everywhere: behind bushes, inside trash cans, up in trees. No one to be seen anywhere. "Who's that singing?" he called out. But no one answered.

He walked on until he again heard:

> *Pink pills for pale people,*
>
> *Pink pills for pale people.*
>
> *Ha, ha, ha, ha, ha.*

The singing seemed to come from overhead. It was a windy day, and the wires waved this way and that. He put his ear to the telephone pole and listened very carefully. Sure enough, the telephone wires and telephone poles were singing "Pink Pills."

As a matter of fact, other people using their telephones began to hear strange voices singing the song and giggling up and down the telephone lines. All of the wires and all of the poles in the country were connected, and from wire to wire and pole to pole and town to town and city to city and state to state, it wasn't long before telephones across the entire nation were echoing with the song:

> *Pink pills for pale people,*
> *Pink pills for pale people.*
> *Ha, ha, ha, ha, ha.*

The lines got to be so noisy that you couldn't hold a decent conversation on the telephone. You would try to talk, but all you would hear was:

> *Pink pills for pale people,*
> *Pink pills for pale people.*
> *Ha, ha, ha, ha, ha.*

The telephone companies and their armies of repairmen could find only one solution to the problem: Rip down all of the wires, put them on a great ship, sail the ship out to the deepest part of the ocean, and dump them.

It was done quickly, and a new telephone system was put in that acted the way wires and poles are supposed to act—just carrying the messages without talking themselves. Everyone was greatly relieved.

But somewhere down in the deepest part of the ocean there's still a great tangle of wires and telephone poles. And every now and then, people who do not believe this story will get into diving suits and go down a half mile below the surface of the ocean to confirm it for themselves! And there they can still hear the wires and poles laughing and singing:

> *Pink pills for pale people,*
> *Pink pills for pale people.*
> *Pink pills, pink pills,*
> *Pink pills for pale people.*
> *Ha, ha, ha, ha, ha!*

Funny how old stories can reflect present-day situations. The Internet via telephone lines can now carry viruses to computers that can cause all sorts of problems in households. Maybe the whole Internet system will have to be scrapped and we'll have to start over—just like in this story. And anyone using a cordless phone—especially within a city—is familiar with overcrowded channels allowing outside conversations to mix in with their own. On some nights, regardless of what kind of telephone you use, it's impossible to even get through to the person you're calling: "All circuits are busy!"

Another reason to leave the phone and computer where they are and go tell a story to your kids.

Keep in mind that updating gender in any of these stories is part of the telling process. In my father's day, most of the doctors and postal carriers were men—but that doesn't mean you have to retell it that way today. You will also notice that we never find out whether the girl gets well or not. We can just assume that she does. It's a good point to remember that when making up stories, it's perfectly all right to wander. Lee Hays used to say that every story needs "a beginning, a muddle, and an end." And I think he's right. In "Pink Pills for Pale People," what starts off as a story about a family, becomes a story about the nation's telephone system. If you wanted, you could go beyond this to a story about the government passing a law against saying things over the phone that are too funny. Or perhaps, the little girl grows up to be a musician like her father and ends up writing a whole concerto for orchestra and telephone wires based upon the tune "Pink Pills." I leave these possibilities up to you.

THE MAGIC COMB

LONG AGO, even if you had very little money, you could still buy split peas—a type of dried pea—for a few pennies. And if you boiled these split peas for a long time you got pea soup. But I'm getting ahead of myself. . . .

A little girl was having a lot of trouble keeping her hair combed and neat. At school, the girl's home economics teacher told her, "I just found some of your hair in the food again. You really must keep your hair combed properly when you come to class. Or you might have to stay home." This upset the girl. She enjoyed the class very much. That afternoon she stopped in at the five-and-ten-cent store and bought herself a new comb.

Although the girl didn't know it, this particular comb happened to be a magic comb.

The next morning she combed her hair and got ready to leave for school.

Her mother said, "Daughter, your hair is combed, but it's so dirty, I do believe you could grow potatoes up there."

The comb must have heard this because when the girl arrived at school—she had stopped along the way to comb her hair one last time—all the other children laughed at her.

"I've combed my hair. What are you laughing at now?" she asked.

"Your hair, your hair! Look at your hair!" they all cried, leaning against one another to keep themselves from falling over from laughter. "You've got potatoes growing in your hair!"

"Oh, that's just what my mother says," said the girl.

"No, there really *are* potatoes," they all said.

"Here, hold still and I'll show you," said one of her class-mates, and he reached into the girl's hair and pulled out a potato.

The girl slowly brought her hand up to rest on her head until she felt something dusty and round. She looked at her reflection in the window. Potatoes filled her hair! She was very embarrassed, but since her first class was home eco-nomics, she plucked the potatoes out of her hair, washed them, and cooked them up. Everyone sat down to enjoy a dish of steaming potatoes.

This still left the problem of *why* potatoes were growing out of her hair. She asked her mother, but her mother only laughed and told her, "Potatoes? In your hair? That's ridiculous. Stop telling stories."

The following day, just before entering the classroom, the girl again combed her hair. And again, all the other children laughed.

"*Now* what are you all laughing at?" she asked her classmates.

"There's spinach growing in your hair!" they said.

"Oh, don't give me that," said the girl as she slowly brought her hand up to rest on what felt like a large spinach patch. "Oh no! Not again!" she cried. She was very embarrassed, but since her first class was home economics, she plucked the spinach out of her hair, washed it, and cooked it up. Everyone sat down to enjoy a dish of steaming spinach. Not cooked too much though, because spinach is best when you cook it just a little.

Well, this got to be the talk of the school. Even the girl's mother was now convinced that there must be something special about a head of hair that produced a different vegetable each day. One day there were carrots, another day onions, on another day beets, lettuce on another. Still other days brought tomatoes or turnips or radishes or Swiss chard or lima beans or green peppers. Several varieties grew out of her head that people had never even tasted before. They consulted seed companies who told them that the vegetables originated overseas, and they had names like Chinese celery and African cabbage.

In fact, the girl began to enjoy the unpredictability of her hair. The other children admired her and boasted about their wonderful classmate who grew vegetables in her hair. Newspaper and television crews camped outside the school grounds hoping to be the first ones to report that day's vegetable. Doctors and universities wrote her letters asking for permission to conduct tests and take samples.

One morning, in a rush to get ready, the girl accidentally stepped on her comb and broke it in two. Without giving it a thought, she threw the pieces in the wastebasket, and on her way to school, stopped in the five-and-ten-cent store to buy a new one.

But the new comb was an ordinary comb, and no vegetable grew out of her hair that day. The magic had disappeared.

She ran right out of school and all the way back home. "It must be the comb," she cried through her tears. She ran into the house, but the wastebasket was empty.

"Oh, darling, I've already taken out the garbage," said her mother. "It's out on the curb." The girl ran outside, but the trash had just been emptied into the garbage truck. The truck was turning the far corner of the block and disappearing out of sight.

The girl chased after it. She was exhausted, but she ran and ran until she finally caught up with the truck just after it dumped the trash at the local landfill. And there, looming in front of her, was a mountain of garbage.

"I've got to find that comb," said the girl. She spent the rest of the day sifting through trash. The garbage had been dumped over a pile of tin cans, empty milk containers, banana peels, and table scraps. A garbageman loaned her a pair of gloves and she pushed aside bottles, chicken bones, old shoes, and all the muck and slime that makes garbage dumps dumpy. Finally, at the bottom of the pile, she found two small plastic pieces. Her magic comb!

She walked back home, cleaned off the broken pieces, and ever so carefully glued them back together, setting the comb aside to dry overnight.

The next morning she got up, combed her hair, and walked to school. But what do you know? From that day on, the only thing that grew out of her hair was split peas.

In these days of canned soups, some children don't know what split peas are. But if split peas are too confusing, one young person suggested substituting banana splits.

And don't get too caught on combs, either. Perhaps your child uses a brush. You can retell this story as "The Magic Brush," or "The Magic Styling Gel," or "The Magic Hair Dryer." As with any story, the possibilities begin and end with you, the storyteller.

THE LITTLE TRAIN

Down at the station

Early in the morning

See the little puffer bellies

All in a row.

See the stationmaster

Pull the little handle,

Toot-toot, puff-puff,

Off they go.

LONG AGO THERE was a little choo-choo train. It was not an electric train. It was not a diesel train. It ran on coal and steam like all trains did in those days.

When the train chugged up a long grade, you could hear

it working very, very hard, *C h o o...c h o o...c h o o... c h o o...* Sometimes the great back wheels would slip. The crew, their faces smeared with soot, would climb down from the engine and walk beside the train, throwing sand on the rails for traction. It was difficult work.

But when the little train rounded the top of a hill, you could hear it speeding up as it started back down, *Choodle doodle, choodle doodle, choodle doodle, choodle doodle...*

On one of its trips the little train went sturdily up and down between pastures and farms until it came to a river. A bridge had once stretched across the river, but a big flood had washed the bridge away. The engineer didn't see this in time and before he could put on the brakes...*keerrrr-plunk!!!* The whole trainload of people landed in the river.

Water came up to the windows!

The engineer turned to the fireman and said, "What'll we do now?"

The fireman turned to the conductor and said, "What'll we do now?"

The conductor turned around, but there wasn't anybody there except the passengers, and they were mad. "Well, I don't know what to do," he whispered.

Just then, a tall old man with long white hair and a long

white beard came striding through the water. In his hand he held a fish spear with three points. On his body he wore a white robe. On his head he wore a crown.

"What seems to be the trouble?" said the old man. He had a fancy old-fashioned way of speaking.

"You derned fool!" said the conductor. "Anybody can see we're stuck!"

"Yes, yes," said the old man, ignoring the conductor's rudeness. "Tell me, Mr. Engineer, what are you using in that engine of yours?"

"We're using coal, of course," interrupted the conductor.

"Well, my friend, then you're the fool!" said the old man with the long white beard. "You're in a river now. You'd better use fish."

And just like that, the old man with the long white beard disappeared.

The engineer turned to the fireman and said, "Did you see what I saw?"

And the fireman turned to the conductor and said, "Did you hear what I heard?"

And the conductor turned around, but there wasn't anyone there except the passengers, and they were mad. "I suppose we might as well try it," he whispered.

"But how will we catch the fish?" asked the fireman.

"Let's see what we can find in the boxcar," said the engineer.

The three men walked back to the boxcar and discovered a whole shipment of brand-new fishing poles. Each man picked up an armload of poles and walked down to the passenger cars.

"Each and every man, woman, and child take one of these fishing poles and stick it out the window like this, see?" shouted out the conductor, sticking the pole out the window and wiggling the line.

It wasn't long before everyone was having a wonderful time catching fish. They caught long fish and short fish. They caught fat fish and thin fish. And what they caught, they handed to the conductor, who carried the fish in coal buckets up to the engineer in the locomotive. The engineer passed the fish to the fireman. The fireman filled the firebox with cool water and threw the fish inside. The fish swam around and around in the firebox, and powered the engine.

"My-oh-my," cried the fireman, "I've never seen her work this well!"

And just as the old man with long white hair and a long

white beard had said it would, the train began to inch forward.

```
FISH . . . . FISH . . . . FISH . . . . FISH,
FISH . . . FISH . . . FISH . . . FISH . . . FISH,
FISH . . FISH . . FISH . . FISH . . FISH . . FISH,
FISHFISHFISHFISH
```

And it chugged on up the river until it got to a smooth, level place on the other side. Then it chugged up the river-bank and back onto the tracks, and continued on its way, FISHFISHFISHFISH, FISHFISHFISHFISH, FISH FISHFISHFISH.

> *Down at the station*
>
> *Early in the morning*
>
> *See the little puffer bellies*
>
> *All in a row.*
>
> *See the stationmaster*
>
> *Pull the little handle,*
>
> *Fish-fish, blub-blub,*
>
> *Off they go.*

I like to start this story off by asking children if they've ever seen an old-fashioned choo-choo train. A choo-choo is fueled by coal and powered by steam, and it is the steam-driven engine that gives the choo-choo its distinctive sound. It's now been fifty years since trains were converted to diesel in this country, and it may well be that a lot of present-day parents have never seen a real choo-choo, except as a tourist attraction or in the movies. By the way, the song in the story is a famous old English tune called "Down at the Station."

Trains, of course, inspired many songs. What an astonishing invention! Think of being able to go twenty-five miles an hour! Why, that's much faster than a horse and wagon could go. But nowadays, many trains have been pushed aside by automobiles. Maybe a new version of "I've Been Working on the Railroad" could be:

I've been working on the highway, all the live long day.

I've been working on the highway, just to pass the time away.

Can't you hear the horns a-honking? It's getting very late.

Can't you see the smog a-rising? How long do I wait?

Yes, times change, and songs and stories can change with them. Today, highway construction often involves a single worker in a big, noisy machine, so it's rare to hear new work songs meant to be sung by a group. But I haven't given up hope yet. Whenever I'm stuck in traffic due to construction, I keep an ear open as I pass the paving crew.

THE OATMEAL POT

A MOTHER AND HER SON lived in a little house on the edge of town. They didn't have much money. Often they were hungry.

"Oh, how I wish I had something to feed my little child," said the mother, looking at the empty cupboard. "Even if it was just plain hot oatmeal."

Suddenly a tiny little man with wings flitted through the window. The window was closed, but he floated right through the glass and made himself comfortable on the kitchen table.

"Greetings, friends! I was flying past and overheard you," said the little man. He waved his hand and out of nowhere a copper pot with a cover appeared on the table. "Now, if you take off this cover and whisper these words into the pot, some delicious hot oatmeal will appear in it." And the little man whispered into the mother's ear two magic words.

"When you've had enough to eat, whisper these magic words to keep the pot from making any more." And he whispered three new words into the mother's ear. Then he whispered them into the little boy's ear. "In case your mother forgets, you should know them, too." Then he fluttered his wings and flew right out the door, even though the door was closed.

The mother looked at her hungry son and said, "Was that a dream? If it was, then why is the pot still sitting here?" The pot looked like any other. They lifted off the cover. There was nothing in it.

"Why don't we test it?" asked the boy.

"Yes, why don't we?" asked the mother. "What harm could it do?" And she whispered the two magic words into the pot. Sure enough, the first magic words started the oatmeal coming right up to the rim.

"Let me stop it," said the boy, and he whispered the three magic words into the pot and stopped it just before it overflowed.

"I guess we'll have to practice making just the right amount," said the mother.

From that day on, she and her son never went hungry (although they sometimes got tired of oatmeal). And because they did not want the neighbors to laugh at them, they never told anyone about their little pot.

One day a jealous neighbor said to himself, "That mother and son don't seem to be going hungry anymore. I wonder why not?" He peeked in their window and saw the woman spooning out a bowl of oatmeal for her son. "Where'd they find the money for oatmeal?" he thought. "They couldn't have bought much—maybe enough oats for a bowl or two."

The next day, the jealous neighbor returned to peek in the window, and again he watched the mother spoon out a bowl of oatmeal. She seemed to be whispering something to the pot before she served the oatmeal. "Maybe she's blowing on it to cool it off," thought the neighbor.

On the third day, the jealous neighbor was sure he would find both the mother and boy sitting in front of empty bowls. After all, they had no money. But when he peeked in the window, he saw the mother whispering to the pot as she had done the day before. Then, to his surprise, she returned for second and third helpings. "How does such a small pot provide so much oatmeal?" he asked himself.

On the fourth day, the neighbor managed to pry the window open just enough to overhear the mother whisper the magic words to start the oatmeal pot. He thought to himself, "This pot can produce as much oatmeal as anybody wants. Enough for thousands, even hundreds of thousands, to eat! If I had it, I could be rich!" He could hardly believe his eyes. But in his excitement, he missed the three magic words to stop the pot!

That night the jealous neighbor crept into the house, picked up the magic pot, and ran away with it to the other side of town. He found an abandoned factory and he whispered the two magic words into the pot. Sure enough, it worked like a charm! The magic words started the oatmeal coming right up to the rim. That night he filled every container he could find with oatmeal. Then he sold them throughout town. Before long, he had enough money to fix up a factory. He hired some workers to fill the containers round-the-clock and other workers to sell them. By now he was making millions of dollars and was known as the Oatmeal King. With his new money he went off on a Mediterranean cruise.

Meanwhile, across town, the poor mother and her son were going hungry again. They thought the little man with wings had taken back his magic pot.

One night, while the Oatmeal King was still away on vacation, the worker on the night shift dozed off. Asleep in his chair, the worker stretched out his legs and unknowingly kicked over the pot. Oatmeal spilled all over and covered up the pot. Soon, there was so much oatmeal that the worker had to flee for his life. There was no way to get back to the pot to set it right. By morning, hot oatmeal covered the first two floors and was spilling out the windows. Oatmeal was flowing down the street like a flood.

At first, people thought it was a joke. But as more and more oatmeal filled the street, the situation became serious. A telegram was sent to the Oatmeal King and he flew back from his vacation. By now, oatmeal had flooded all the streets and buildings and was filling the valley like a river.

On the other side of town, the woman and the boy realized what must have happened to their little pot. "I can't believe someone would steal food from our mouths," said the mother.

They ran to the police and said, "We know where all the oatmeal is coming from!"

The police pushed them aside. "So does he," said the police commander, pointing to a white limousine that had just arrived. "Make way for the Oatmeal King! Move aside."

"Oh, this is terrible, terrible, terrible!" cried the Oatmeal King, getting out of his fancy car.

"Just shut the pot off," said the commander.

"Shut it off? I don't know how to shut it off. I just know how to start it," said the Oatmeal King.

"What are we supposed to do?" said the commander. "It's your pot and I'm holding you responsible."

By now, the whole town was nothing but a deep lake of steaming hot oatmeal. Somewhere at the bottom was the oatmeal pot, but now nobody knew how to find it. The Oatmeal King tried getting into a diving suit to go down, but the lake was too hot. "Find my old neighbors, the mother and her little boy," he gasped. "They must know how to shut it off."

This time the police listened to the mother and the little boy. The mother said, "Unless we stop the pot, it will keep making hot oatmeal until the whole world is nothing but oatmeal. It'll fill up the sky until the moon and the stars drown in oatmeal. We have got to stop it!"

The mayor of the town asked the mother, "What shall we do? Do you know how to shut the pot off?"

"Of course we do. It's our pot," said the mother. "The problem is how to find it."

The little boy spoke up. "Get me an icebox! Then lower me down into the lake. I'll find it."

So that's what they did. They closed the boy in the icebox and lowered him on a cable. Down at the bottom of the oatmeal lake he found his way to the overflowing pot. He opened the icebox door just long enough to shout the three magic words.

It was a narrow escape. As it was, the entire world had to eat oatmeal for a year just to get rid of the mess. But it taught everybody a good lesson.

You mean you're going to ask how the little boy maneuvered in a closed icebox? The same way the wolf swallowed Little Red Riding Hood in one gulp. Only grown-ups ask silly questions like that.

"The Oatmeal Pot" is my father's version of the old story about a person who steals a magic salt mill. Salt was very precious in ancient times and in some places a pound of salt was as valuable as a pound of gold. Salt in its natural form comes in a large block, so you needed a salt mill to grind it up. But this particular salt mill was magic: It kept producing salt, and more salt, as long as you said the magic words. Then the salt mill was stolen, put on a ship, and fell overboard right down to the bottom

of the ocean. And it kept on churning out salt. That's why the ocean is so salty today.

Each culture seems to have its own story of the overflowing pot. In Japan, it's an overflowing pot of rice. In Italy, it's an overflowing pot of pasta. My father just made up his own version, or perhaps he heard it from somebody else and retold it with a little embellishment.

Either way, grab a bowl, a spoon, a little brown sugar, some butter, maybe a few raisins, and enjoy!

2 *New Versions of Old Stories*

ONE OF THE earliest lessons I received in storytelling came, naturally enough, from a teacher.

I was eight years old and had arrived late at boarding school. "Are you going to listen to Mrs. Curtis tonight?" my friends asked me. "She's telling us *Treasure Island* in the library."

That night a dozen of us gathered on the rug in the small library. Mrs. Curtis took a seat on the couch with several kids at her side. The only light came from the fireplace. First, she reminded us where she had left off the night before. Then, without the aid of a book or notes, she began telling a chapter of Robert Louis Stevenson's exciting adventure story. She seemed to have the whole book memorized!

The next day I asked Mrs. Curtis, "How do you remember all those words?" She laughed. "I don't remember it word for word," she said. "I've told this story many times, but if I need to refresh my memory, I brush up on a chapter earlier in the day. Then, I retell it in my own words in the evening."

A quarter of a century later, I tried this technique with my own kids' bedtime stories. At the time, we still lived in a cabin with no electricity. Sitting there in the dark, I tried to retell old movies or plays I had seen or novels I had read. Or

I would leaf through a book of fables or fairy tales while it was still daylight, then retell one or two that evening, just like Mrs. Curtis.

The advantage to retelling old stories is that it's hard to make them fail, even if you are new to storytelling. Classics like "Goldilocks and the Three Bears" or "The Tortoise and the Hare" have lasted for centuries because they're basically very entertaining. They've also stuck around because they can be appreciated on several levels. Bounce the experience of life against a good story, and it bounces back new meanings.

But don't limit yourself to fables and fairy tales. There are all kinds of books out there. I like the Bible because its stories tend to give the plot but leave the details up to you. The Bible doesn't tell us whether Moses was fat or skinny or how Noah fed all the animals on the ark. And many of its stories are so brief, they almost demand to be fleshed out with dialogue and description.

For instance, with "David and Goliath," I like to add a scene involving David's parents: "Are you out of your mind, David?" say his parents. "You can't beat Goliath. You can't swing a big sword. You're not even growing a beard yet." David says, "I don't need a big sword. I've got my sling. I can kill a wolf on the opposite side of a field. Goliath will be a much easier target. Besides, I have the strength of the Lord in this arm." And he looks at his parents so intently, they are convinced. Obviously, this is some little kid. So they allow him to go. But parents can't help being parents: "Don't forget to look both ways," they call after him.

Many ancient stories are full of death and danger because life was dangerous. If you didn't run fast enough a large animal could catch you for supper. Or, I suppose, a small animal could outrun you, and you'd end up with no supper yourself. Daily existence was a trial for our ancestors. You obeyed the rules of the tribe or you were out. The stories they told reflected this.

Daily life today is perhaps safer, but is much more complex. Just think of all the choices at our fingertips: what to buy at the supermarket, what to read at the library, even where to live. No doubt this is why the modern world is so confusing for young people. "How do we know what's wrong and what's right?" they ask. Luckily, we have stories to help us help them. And if we adults do our job, we'll learn to tell the stories that respond to their questions and to adapt the classics to fit new challenges.

So here, in this section, are my versions of a few old favorites.

NOAH AND THE ARK

NOBODY IS SO BAD that they don't have some good in them. And nobody is so good that they don't have some bad in them. But this is a story about a man who proved to be the exception. His name was Noah, and he was one hundred percent good.

"Why can't more people be like Noah?" the Lord asked himself. "Why is there so much wickedness in the world? Did I make a mistake somewhere?" And he decided that all people, all creatures, large and small, should be drowned in a great flood. All except for Noah.

So the Lord came to Noah as if in a dream and said, "There's going to be rain like never before. Build a huge boat, an ark, and when all the earth is flooded, you and your family will stay afloat."

Noah sat up in bed. "An ark?" he said. "I don't know how to build an ark. I'm only a farmer, and besides, I'm six hundred years old."

"Do not worry," said the Lord. "I will tell you how." And he gave Noah exact instructions on how high, wide, and long the ark should be: what kind of wood to use, and how to shape the wood, and how to coat it with pitch—both inside and out—so the boat wouldn't leak.

Then the Lord said, "Bring on board two each of all living creatures—one female and one male—so they can live, too. This goes for lions and tigers. This goes for mice and kangaroos."

Now, it took a big boat to hold all these animals and reptiles and insects and birds, a very fat kind of boat. In fact, the ark looked more like a building than a boat. It didn't need the usual mast with a sail because it didn't have to go anyplace. It just had to float.

So Noah and his family collected two cats, two dogs, two cows, two sheep, two elephants, two deer, two raccoons, two fleas, two mosquitoes, two bumblebees, and two of all the other animals and reptiles and insects and birds in the world.

Big as it was, it was still a crowded ark!

And noisy, too! All those barks and roars and meows and

peeps and quacks and snorts and buzzings made quite a racket. And as soon as Noah got two of everything on board, the rain started to come down . . .

and down . . .

and down.

It rained long and hard. First there were puddles. Then swollen rivers. Then floods. And it wasn't long before the ark began to float.

It rained for one night.

Then all the next day.

And all the next night.

Then all the next day.

For forty days and forty nights it rained. All the valleys, then the hills—even the tallest mountains—were covered by water. Only Noah, his family, and the animals on the ark survived.

Finally, the rain stopped. But the earth was still flooded. Noah waited and waited until one day he opened the window of his ark and sent out a dove. "Little dove, please look for land," he said. But the dove soon returned because there was no land to rest on.

After seven days Noah again released the dove. It returned that evening with an olive branch in its mouth. "Little dove, the tops of trees must be above-water," said Noah.

He waited seven more days and released the dove again. This time the dove did not return. "It found dry land," said Noah. And it wasn't long before Noah could see a towering mountain in the distance. And this is where the ark eventually came to rest, on the side of Mount Ararat.

Then a beautiful sight appeared to Noah, a rainbow with all its many colors. "It's a sign of peace," said Noah. "Like the rainbow, we are all different, but we are also one."

"Noah," said the Lord, "you are a wise and good man. I will never again flood the earth. So go forth, be fruitful, and multiply."

The world in the story of Noah is not the same world we live in today. But that will not be difficult for children to understand. A boat can become a floating farm, a man can be six hundred years old, and if you add a few elephants, cats, frogs, snakes, skunks, tigers, and toads, kids are going to pay attention.

Just think of the infinite stories that might arise when all of these creatures go on a cruise together. What is daily life like? There's probably a lot of grumbling. "Not enough food with all these animals," the turtle complains. Then the cat suggests, "Let's

do some fishing." But the zebra complains, "I don't like fish."
Maybe the chickens donate some eggs and the cows some milk?
It's obvious that Noah will have to be a great mediator.

With this in mind, the dove with the olive branch, and later
the rainbow, must have been very hopeful signs for the passen-
gers on the ark. The rainbow is still a powerful symbol for differ-
ent opinions existing side by side. It means you don't have to get
all blurred and mixed-up in order to come together. You can be
yourself. The red stripe is red, the green stripe is green, the blue
stripe is blue. They are separate, but when they come together,
they create one of nature's most stunning visual effects.

In more recent history, African slaves made a verse out of the
last part of the story. It's a verse that's used in gospel song after
gospel song. I'd say it's one of the greatest lines in all of American
folk music. "God gave Noah the rainbow sign, no more water, but
fire next time." In other words, if we can't learn to get along to-
gether, there's going to be real trouble.

The symbol of the rainbow is not only found in gospel songs.
Just take "Over the Rainbow" from the movie, The Wizard of
Oz. *The lyrics were written by my friend Yip Harburg. You know*
the words, right? About finding a land over the rainbow? It's a
wonderful song—the rainbow is a place of hope, happiness, and
peace—but I've found that I have to make a small change when

I'm singing it onstage. (I can hear Yip saying, "Pete, you can fool around with your old folk songs, but don't you touch 'Over the Rainbow.'") Yip, wherever you are, I have to add two words. If I'd been there when Dorothy was singing, wondering why she couldn't find the land over the rainbow, I'd tell her, "You know why you can't? Because you're only asking for yourself. You've got to ask for everybody. So sing it, 'Why can't you and I?'"

Either we're all going to make it over the rainbow or nobody's going to.

JONAH AND THE WHALE

GOD NEEDED A PROPHET, somebody to carry His word forward.

He went to Jonah. "Jonah," said God. "You are the son of Amittai. Rise and go to the great city of Nineveh. It is full of sinners. Preach to them that I have become aware of their wickedness."

"Lord," said Jonah, "I don't want the job. It's dangerous. It's a lot of work. And besides, Nineveh is far away. Can't you just set them all on fire or something?"

"No, I want to give them a chance," said God. "And I am giving you the job. So get up, Jonah. Go to Nineveh."

But Jonah grumbled to himself, "I'm not going. I'll slip away from the Lord. I'll get on a ship bound for the far land of Tarshish, the kingdom at the end of the world. The Lord will never catch up to me there."

So Jonah went down to the port in Joppa, paid his fare, and set sail for Tarshish. But Jonah should have known he couldn't get away from the Lord so easily.

No sooner was the ship at sea than a terrible storm blew in and threatened to break the ship apart. The crew had never seen such a storm. Each sailor prayed to his own god for safekeeping. In those days sailors came from different parts of the world, just as they do today. And in those days sailors had different names for God, just as many of us do today.

Now you might be wondering where Jonah was during all of this commotion. Would you believe that he had snuck below deck to find himself a nice, comfortable place to sleep? And he'd found one, too, on some sacks of grain right near what sailors call the "ceiling." But be aware that on a sailing ship the ceiling is not above your head. It's the side part, inside the ribs where the planks go. A ship has lots of different names like this. You don't go downstairs on a ship, you go *below deck*. You don't go upstairs on a ship, you go *above deck*. And when you go up the mast, you go *aloft*.

And it was below deck, against the ceiling, that the ship's mate discovered Jonah curled up and snoring. "Hey, you there!" said the ship's mate, shaking Jonah awake. "What do you mean by sleeping? This ship is going to sink if we don't all help out. Pray to your god for safekeeping."

"Uh-oh," said Jonah to himself.

"Follow me, you lazy landlubber," said the mate, and he led Jonah above deck to where the ship's crew had gathered. "Hey, lads! Look who I found sleeping below deck."

"Well, you're just in time," said the ship's captain to Jonah. "We're drawing straws. Blame for this storm lies with the man who draws the shortest one."

"Uh-oh," said Jonah again. He knew he would draw the shortest straw. And he did.

"What's the meaning of this?" yelled the crew. "First, we catch you below deck; now you draw the shortest straw."

"I . . . I . . . I . . . ," said Jonah, trying to get the words out.

"C'mon, tell us the truth," they said. "Who are you? Where do you come from?"

"I am a Hebrew," said Jonah finally. "I worship the Lord, the God of heaven who made the sea and the land."

"And are you the person to blame for this storm?"

"Yes," said Jonah. "It is God's way of punishing me."

"Punishing you? What did you do?" asked the sailors, now frightened by his words.

"The Lord wants me to go to Nineveh and preach to its sinners. But I don't want to be a preacher. I don't want to be a prophet. I thought I could escape," said Jonah.

"Well, how are we supposed to stop this storm?" asked the crew.

"Throw me overboard," said Jonah. "Only then will calm weather return."

The ship's crew didn't want to throw him overboard. They thought it might make Jonah's god even angrier. But the storm only got worse.

First, stronger wind.

Then, louder thunder.

Then, brighter lightning.

Then, higher waves.

"OK! We give up," the crew cried out. "We'll throw this Jonah overboard, but don't blame us if he drowns. It won't be our fault." And they picked Jonah up by his hands and his legs and—swing, swing, *S-W-I-N-G!* They threw him high, out over the water. *S-P-L-A-S-H!* went Jonah into the sea.

And all at once, the wind stopped blowing.

The thunder stopped booming.

The lightning stopped crackling.

And the waves stopped crashing.

And that was the end of the ship's troubles. The rest of the journey was smooth sailing. But Jonah's troubles were just beginning. He sank down toward the bottom of the ocean and along the way, he was swallowed . . . by an unsuspecting whale.

Now, whales do have to swallow a lot of junk. But it's one thing to swallow tiny things like krill and plankton, and quite another thing to swallow a prophet. Jonah didn't like being down in the whale's stomach, either. He complained the whole time and made a ruckus. He stamped his feet. He hollered. He bellowed. Admittedly, the whale's stomach was smelly. And occasionally, the whale would burp. What a sound! Its whole body shook like an earthquake.

For three days and for three nights, Jonah remained in the belly of the whale. Then the Lord's voice came down to Jonah and said, "Are you going to do what I told you to do?"

"I'll do it, Lord," said Jonah. "I realize I can't escape from you. I've been down here for such a long time. Please, get me out of here."

So the Lord said, "Whale, swim toward Nineveh. Come up close to the beach. Spit him out on the sand. Don't hurt him, though."

And that's just what the whale did. He spit Jonah onto shore as gently as possible. Jonah staggered up the beach.

"Jonah, aren't you forgetting something?" said the Lord.

"What?" said Jonah. He heard a *harrumph* behind him. It was the whale. "You mean, I have to thank this fish for its smelly ride?"

"Jonah!" scolded the Lord.

"OK, OK." Jonah looked at the whale. "Thank you, whale."

"That's better," said the Lord. "Now, Jonah, do your duty."

And this time Jonah did his duty, but that is another story.

Long ago, trips and adventures like this were the standard fare for storytelling. Think of the stories of Moses in the desert or

Odysseus at sea; they are stories about people traveling and how they get to where they want to go. Even fairy tales are often about people taking trips: A person goes into unknown territory and finally gets back home, be it by wit, magic, luck, or faith.

In the Bible the story of Jonah and the whale is very short, close to being just a description. This leaves plenty of room for embellishment. Imagine the smell of the salt air as the sailors left the port of Joppa or the sway of the ship during the great storm. Ask yourself what you would do if you were stuck inside a whale. Or put yourself in the whale's place for a moment. How would you react to Jonah? A friend of mine, Jim Forest, wrote a wonderful picture book, A Whale's Tale, *from the point of view of the whale. One of the pictures shows the whale swallowing Jonah with the line "Prophets are hard to swallow."*

So if you're comfortable telling Bible stories, why not try "Moses in the Bulrushes" from the viewpoint of the pharaoh's daughter? Or what if you were a news reporter covering the battle between David and Goliath or the adventure of Daniel in the lions' den? The Bible is filled with tales that can fit the story-telling needs of just about anybody.

Of course, some biblical stories are retold so often that their characters become part of our commonly used vocabulary. Ever since Jonah was thrown overboard, sailors have used his name for one who brings bad luck to a ship. The crew says, "So you're the Jonah bringing us bad luck? We should throw you overboard."

But perhaps the greater legacy left by Jonah was his mistaken belief that if he got far enough away, he could ignore his responsibilities. Like Jonah, we need to face up to our duty. It is up to us to bring our neighborhoods and our world to a place of balance and peace.

FOOLISH HANS

HANS WAS A STRONG young man. One day his mother said, "Hans, you're twenty-one. Do you ever think of getting married?"

"Huh, Ma?" said Hans.

"Isn't there a girl who appeals to you?" she asked.

"Well, I've seen Elsa at church. She looks like a hard worker," said Hans. Elsa lived with her family across the valley.

"So go court her," said his mother.

"Huh? What do ya mean, Ma?"

"Go visit her. Bring her a present. Our cow just had a calf. Take the calf and give it to Elsa."

Now Hans was *very* strong. With little effort, he swung the calf up around his neck and carried it across the valley two miles, all the way to Elsa's house. He arrived at her door covered in sweat and dirt.

"Elsa! I've come a-courtin'. I've brought you a present," called Hans.

"Oh, Hans, a calf! That's a wonderful present. Thank you, but why didn't you put a string around its neck and lead it here? There was no need to carry it," said Elsa.

"Huh? I never thought of that. That's a good idea. I'll remember that. Bye, Elsa!" And he turned and left as quickly as he had arrived.

The next Sunday came. And again, Hans's mother asked, "Hans, aren't you going to visit Elsa today?"

"Huh? I guess so. Sure."

"You should bring her a present. I just baked some bread. Take her a loaf."

Hans was about to start off when he said, "Oops, I almost forgot." He got a string from the barn, tied it around the bread, and dragged the loaf down the dusty road, across the valley two miles, all the way to Elsa's house.

"Elsa! I've come a-courtin'. I've brought you a present," called Hans.

"Oh, Hans, a loaf of bread! Thank you, but why didn't

you put it under your hat to keep the dust off it? I'm afraid it's not good to eat after being dragged across the valley."

"Huh? I never thought of that. That's a good idea. I'll re-member that. Bye, Elsa!" And he turned and left as quickly as he had arrived.

The next Sunday came. And again Hans's mother asked, "Hans, aren't you going to visit Elsa today?"

"Huh? I guess so. Sure."

"You should bring her a present. I just churned some butter. Take her some."

Hans was about to start off when he said, "Oops, I al-most forgot." He took off his hat, placed the butter on top of his head, and put his hat back on. It was a hot day, and he walked across the valley two miles, all the way to Elsa's house.

When he arrived, melted butter dripped down his face. "Elsa! I've come a-courtin'. I've brought you a present," called Hans. He took off his hat, but the butter was half its original size.

Elsa could only sigh. "Hans, I don't think you better come courting again," she said. "I feel you'd be better off courting somebody else."

"Huh, Elsa? But I did what you told me."

"I know, Hans, but just the same. And you better take your calf back, too. I wouldn't feel right keeping her. She's in the barn."

"OK, if you say so, Elsa," said Hans, and he walked out to the barn to fetch the calf. But by this time, the butter had dripped into his eyes, and Hans could barely see. Foolishly, he picked up a donkey instead of the calf. "Jeepers," said Hans. "Elsa sure has fattened you up, little calf. I don't have a string with me so I hope you don't mind being carried again." And with a loud grunt, Hans swung the donkey up around his neck, and set awkwardly off for home.

"*EEE-awww,*" brayed the donkey. "*EEE-awww, EEE-awww.*"

"Gosh, little calf, you don't sound too well," said Hans. "But don't worry, I'll have you home in no time." And off they went in a rather crooked fashion.

Back in town, there lived a mayor who had only one child, a lovely daughter. But there was a problem. She was too serious. He couldn't get her to laugh at anything.

One day the daughter became ill. Her face grew pale and

she lost her appetite. Doctors were called from every direction to offer their advice.

"Have her eat more apples," proclaimed one doctor.

"Have her wake before sunrise and go to sleep before
sunset," proclaimed another. The mayor patiently tried each
doctor's remedy, but nothing worked.

Finally, the old village nurse came to the house. "Good
nurse, what shall I do?" pleaded the mayor. "What good is
governing a town if I cannot help my own daughter?"

"Well, it's easy to see that this girl is far too serious," proclaimed the nurse. "It's making her sick. Find somebody to
make her laugh and do it quick."

So the mayor sent his assistants out far and wide. He
posted a notice in the town hall. He made an announcement in the village square: "Hear ye, hear ye. A sack of gold
to anyone who can make my daughter laugh."

Over the next few days clowns and jugglers and comedians and actors arrived at the house, eager to perform in
front of the mayor's daughter. The chance to win a sack of
gold did not come along often. But none of the performers
could bring even a smile to the daughter's lips. She only
looked at them sadly, then returned to her room to lie
down.

The mayor once again called upon the village nurse. "Stop wasting time," the nurse scolded. "Obviously a sack of gold is not enough. Your daughter must laugh or she'll not see the end of the year."

The mayor hurried to his daughter's room. "Daughter, I'm at my wit's end. Tell me what to do."

"I don't know, Father," she said weakly. "But if somebody could make me laugh, I'd marry him on the spot."

The next day the mayor sent his assistants out far and wide. He posted a notice at the town hall. He made an announcement in the village square: "Hear ye, hear ye. My daughter's hand in marriage to anyone who can make her laugh."

Once again, clowns and jugglers and comedians and actors arrived at the house eager to perform in front of the mayor's daughter. The chance to marry the daughter of a mayor did not come along often. But none of the performers could bring even a smile to the daughter's lips. She only looked at them sadly, then returned to her room to lie down. "I must rest my eyes," she said.

But now . . . who should come stumbling through the village, making a terrible racket?

"What is that noise?" the daughter cried. She went to the

window, ready to scold the culprit. But there she saw the half-blind Hans, slowly zigzagging up the street, butter dripping down his face, a braying donkey slung around his neck.

One look at this spectacle and the daughter began to giggle, and giggle a little more, and then she laughed. She laughed so uproariously, her father came running into the room.

"Daughter, you're laughing!" cried the mayor.

"Ha, ha, Father. Come, look—ha, ha—out the window."

The mayor took one look at Hans and he, too, could not keep from laughing. "Ha, ha. That man is a genius!" he declared. "And strong, too. He'll make a fine husband!"

And so it was that Foolish Hans married the mayor's daughter.

Earlier I talked about my father's stories, but this is one that my mother told me. When she told this famous old German story, it ended after Elsa turned Hans down. But if "Foolish Hans" ends with Elsa's rejection, we might see only the cautionary side of the tale—Don't apply last week's solution to this week's situation.

Years later, I heard a similar story involving a rich man's daughter who gets sick because she refuses to laugh. In this version, I put the two together and Hans is eventually rewarded for just being himself, foolish as he might be.

I've thrown in a few other changes as well. For instance, I don't like the idea that if you marry the rich person—the prince or the princess—all of your troubles will be solved. Too many fairy tales end like this. So in place of the rich man, I've used a mayor. This isn't a drastic departure from the original theme—there's still a lovely girl, marriage, and an offer of gold—but it's a start. And while some of you may feel more comfortable keeping with tradition, I hope others will decide to change it even further.

STONE SOUP

A LONG, LONG TIME AGO, there was a war. And after the war, there was a famine, which means there wasn't enough food for everyone to eat. Imagine not eating for one day. Imagine not eating for two days. Imagine not eating for three days!

Well, it so happened that a soldier, trying to make his way back home on foot, hadn't eaten for four days!

He arrived at a village and knocked on the first door he came to: *Knock! Knock! Knock!* An old woman answered the door.

"Can you spare a bite to eat?" the soldier asked. "I'm starving."

"*You're* hungry?" the old woman said. "This whole village is hungry. The war has robbed us of everything. Look in the fields. Are there cows out there? Horses? Sheep? They've all been stolen by soldiers. Knock on any door you want. You'll get the same answer."

So the soldier knocked on a few more doors, and sure enough, he got the same answer.

"Food?" said one old man. "Don't you know there's a famine? Get away from here."

"Food?" said a young woman in the next house. "I have none. My own children are out gathering grass right now."

"Grass?" said the soldier. "That's what animals eat."

"Well, they can't very well eat stones, can they?" said the woman, and she shut the door and locked it.

The soldier was too hungry to argue, but the woman had given him an idea. He walked down to the village well where some villagers were filling their pails with water. "Mmmm, stones," said the soldier.

"What?" said the man next to him.

"Stones," he said. "I'm going to make stone soup."

"Poor thing, you're crazy from hunger," said a woman.

"I am not," declared the soldier. "Stone soup is delicious!"

"Until the stones break your teeth," said a boy, giggling to himself.

"Not if you cook them," said the soldier.

"Cook them?" some other children asked.

The soldier had to think quickly now. "Of course," he said. "You mean to tell me, no one here has ever tasted stone soup?"

The villagers thought he was joking. "A soup from stones?" they asked.

"Of course," said the soldier. "Get me some stones like this, and I'll show you." And he held out a stone the size of a fist. "Nice, smooth, round ones."

The children ran off and got the stones, which the soldier carefully washed. He was beginning to attract a crowd of curious onlookers.

"Now I need a big pot," said the soldier. "The biggest one you can carry." The children again ran off and came back with a pot so big, it had to be carried by three large boys.

"What's this all about?" the boys asked.

"This soldier says he's going to make a soup from stones," said the crowd.

"What kind of trick is that?" said the boys, setting the pot down.

The soldier said nothing. He built a fire, then busied

himself filling the pot with water, pail after pail. He added the stones one at a time. "Mmmm, this is a good one," he said, licking a stone, then dropping it in.

After the water came to a boil, the soldier tasted it and said, "Mmmm, if only it had some salt."

One boy said, "I know where I can find some salt." And he ran off and came back with some.

The soldier added the salt and tasted the soup. "Mmmm," he said. "If only it had a bone or two."

One old woman said, "Well, we don't have much, but our family could spare a bone." She tapped her grandson on the arm, and he ran off and came back with one.

"Mmmm," said the soldier, after adding the bone. "This is going to be one of my best stone soups."

"Let us taste it," said the crowd.

"No, it's not quite ready. If only it had some onions."

"Well, we don't have much, but our family could spare some onions," said a girl, and she ran off and came back with some onions.

And after a half an hour, the soup started to smell good. The soldier tasted it. "Mmmm, delicious," he said. "But if only it had a few potatoes."

"Well, we don't have much, but our family could spare

some potatoes," said a little girl, and she ran off and came back with some potatoes.

And as the afternoon wore on, every time somebody asked to taste the soup, the soldier would say, "If only it had a few carrots. . . . If only it had a little barley. . . ."

By this time, the smell of the soup had spread around the whole village, and the soldier knew he couldn't hold the villagers off much longer. "OK," he said, "everybody get your bowls and spoons."

And the whole hungry village shared stone soup.

"I must have your recipe," said one woman.

"The stones really do make a difference," said a little boy.

I first heard "Stone Soup" told by my friend Jo Schwartz, and I've told "Stone Soup" onstage now for thirty years. On the one hand, it's a story about a soldier saved by his own wits; on the other, it's about the miraculous things that happen when people work to-gether. Each contributes some small part of the soup, and they end up with more than they put in.

Of course, when people don't want to share, they hoard what little they have, and then scarcity really does set in. But when people work together, there's no telling what can be accomplished. You might find examples of "stone soup" in your town or city. A community-built playground is one that comes to mind. One person has the tire. One person has the wood. Another has the tools. Another has the knowledge. Then, one day, everyone comes together, and before you know it, there is a wonderful playground. The world is a big stone; it's what we bring to it that counts.

THE BOY WHO DREW CATS

LONG AGO, there was a hardworking farmer. He wanted his son to be the same. After all, it takes more than one person to keep a farm running smoothly.

But the boy preferred to draw pictures.

"Where's that boy now?" the father would ask while hard at work in the fields. The boy, stick in hand, could be found at the field's edge, drawing pictures in the dirt.

Finally, the father told his son, "You're a good-for-nothing. Here I am, hard at work, trying to teach you how to farm, and you just draw pictures. You never do anything. I'm going to apprentice you to a man in town. Then you'll either work or get punished."

Early the next day, the father brought the son to a shop-keeper down in the village. "Make him work hard," the father said. "If he slacks off, punish him. Or send him back to me. I'll fix him."

Despite the threats of punishment, it wasn't long before the boy began drawing at his new job. The shop had some beautiful inks and brushes for painting signs. And while the shopkeeper wasn't looking, the boy would swipe a brush and dip it into the beautiful inks. In fact, he enjoyed drawing with a brush even more than with a stick. The shopkeeper would punish him, but the boy continued to draw.

He drew on anything he could find: storeroom walls, packing crates, linens hanging on the line. And he especially loved to draw pictures of cats. Cats climbing trees. Cats chasing butterflies. Cats sleeping in the sun.

One day, after the boy had drawn a cat right on the front of the store, the shopkeeper got fed up. "You're a good-for-nothing. Here I am, hard at work, trying to teach you a skill, and you just draw pictures. Go on back to your father! Go!"

"OK. But shouldn't I first wash out your brush?"

"Take the brush for all I care. Just get out."

Of course, returning home was no choice at all. "I can't go home," the boy said to himself. "Father will just punish me."

So he took the first road that led in the opposite direction.

He walked,

   and walked,

      and walked all day.

He was growing tired, and the sky looked like rain. Where could he spend the night? Or find some food? On one side of the road there was a big rice paddy where workers were busy planting rice. Across the paddy, he could just make out the outline of a small temple. Maybe the priests would allow him to work in exchange for food and shelter.

He stopped and asked a group of workers, "Do you think they'd let me stay in that temple overnight?"

"They? Who's they?" asked an old man.

"The priests, of course," said the boy.

"There's no one in that temple anymore," said a younger man. "It's haunted. You'd better not go there."

"But it's going to rain," the boy said.

"Better to get wet!" another worker said. "The last man who went in there was never seen again!"

"Oh, you're just trying to scare me," said the boy. "I'll find out for myself." And he set out, balancing himself on the little footpaths through the rice paddy. In no time at all, he was knocking at the temple door.

Knock, knock, knock. No answer.

Knock, knock, knock. No answer.

He pushed on the door. It opened very slowly. *EEEkkk,* went the door, as though the hinges needed oiling. The temple was deserted. Cobwebs were everywhere. The boy felt so alone, he wanted to draw.

He could just make out a little fireplace where there had been some kind of altar. There were bits of charcoal left over from the last fire. He picked up a piece of the charcoal and pressed it against the wall. It made a mark. He couldn't resist the temptation and began drawing cats. The more he drew, the better he felt. He drew great big cats all over the temple walls, each cat more excited and ferocious than the last. Some of the cats had great big teeth. Some of the cats had great big claws. But after a while the sun started to set and the boy grew tired. He curled up in a corner of the temple and fell into a deep sleep.

During the night, the boy was suddenly awakened by loud, terrible noises. He heard something snarling, *Rrrooaarr! Rrrooaarr!* Then he heard something else snarling and scratching, *Mrrrrrrrrrhrrrhrr! Mrrrrrrrrrhrrrhrr!* Then he heard something pouncing and the sounds of a struggle.

Crash!

Thump!

Thud!

The boy squeezed himself into the corner as tightly as he could.

Mrrrrrrrrrhrrrhrr! Rrrooaarr!

It was so dark he couldn't see a thing, but the sounds were deafening, as if strange, huge animals were fighting right there in the temple. He could feel their hot breath filling the room. The boy squeezed himself even farther into the corner. He had never been so frightened.

Then, just as suddenly as it had begun, the snarling and the roaring stopped. The boy lay as still as possible in the dark for what seemed like hours until the sun began to rise. As the sky lightened, he could make out a strange, huge thing in the middle of the temple floor.

It was as big as a horse, but it wasn't a horse!

It was as big as a cow, but it wasn't a cow!

It didn't move. The boy cautiously got to his feet. He walked around it. Its eyes were half open. Its mouth was half open. It was an enormous *rat*!

And it was dead.

But something else about the temple seemed different. The boy looked at the walls. Could his eyes be playing tricks on him? The cats he had drawn the night before were no longer just black charcoal against white walls.

Their faces were red with blood!

He stood there half stunned, unable to say a word. Finally, he said, "Thank you, cats. You saved my life."

He walked out of the temple and across the rice paddy, past the workers with their mouths hanging open in surprise. "You're alive!" they called after him, but he didn't stop. Instead he pointed with his finger, as though they should look in the temple for themselves. Then he kept on walking.

In a few days the boy arrived in a large city. Unable to pay for lodging the first night, he slept in the park. The next morning he awoke to find an old man sitting beside him, painting. "I noticed you have a brush," the old man said to him. "You must be an artist, too."

"I'm not sure," said the boy, rubbing the sleep from his eyes. "I mean, I do like to draw."

"Well then," said the old man, smiling, "you're just the person I've been looking for." The old man was a painter, the kind who paints pictures on walls and cloth. He needed an apprentice to mix his inks and paints.

Years later, the boy became a well-known painter himself. But he also liked to tell stories, especially the one about a boy who drew cats.

When I was seven or eight years old, my mother showed me a beautiful Japanese picture book printed on rice paper. The paper was as thin as tissue paper, but much stronger, with print on only one side. The pages of the book were connected at both edges like a big accordion, so when you turned one page, you actually turned two.

The name of the book was The Boy Who Drew Cats. I also liked to draw, and this was a fantastic story—a boy saved by his own artistic creations. I like stories that show how art can change lives, where art, not money, is what saves the poor boy or girl from a life of drudgery.

Of course, as the teller, feel free to change things around to fit your audience's own interests. Maybe you have a little girl and she wants the story to begin in the city and end in the country. Maybe she wants to be an architect instead of a painter. Do whatever you like to make the story come alive.

THE TWO FROGS

THERE WERE ONCE two frogs. One was a so-be-it frog. It always said, "That's the way things are. We can't change them." The second was a why-is-it frog. It always said, "Why are things this way? Can't we change them?"

The two frogs lived in a pond near a big dairy farm. And one evening, they were hopping along when they came across a tall can of milk with its cover left off. Earlier, the farmer had sold some of the milk to his neighbors, but he had forgotten to cover the milk and store it away for safekeeping.

Back in those days, farmers kept their milk in tall, forty-eight-quart cans, which were called "hundred weights." Usually a farmer had a cold spring with a little house around it—a springhouse—where he stored the milk overnight. The cool water kept the milk fresh until morning when it could be trucked off to the creamery.

"I wonder what's in that can?" said the so-be-it frog.

"Yes, I wonder, too?" said the why-is-it frog. They were both curious.

Well, the two frogs hopped into the can. *S-p-l-a-s-h!* went the so-be-it frog. *S-p-l-a-s-h!* went the why-is-it frog. But because the tall can was only half full, the two frogs soon discovered that they couldn't hop out. Nighttime was fast approaching. The farmer was going to bed. And after thrashing around a bit, the two frogs were both about to drown.

The so-be-it frog said, "There's no hope." And with one last gurgle he sank to the bottom.

The why-is-it frog said, "Hey, wait! Are you sure there's no hope? There must be some other way."

The why-is-it frog kept on splashing . . .

    and splashing and kicking . . .

    and kicking and splashing.

In the morning, the farmer woke up and said, "Uh-oh! I left that half can of milk out last night." And he ran out to the barn without even bothering to change out of his pajamas.

And what do you think he found?

One tired but very alive frog sitting on top of a big cake of butter.

It pays to kick.

There's hardly a story in this book that can't be made longer or shorter. I originally heard this tale as a forty-second anecdote. It went something like this:

> *A farmer once left a tall can of milk with the top off outside his door. Two frogs hopped into it, then found that they couldn't hop out. After thrashing around a bit, one of them said, "There's no hope." With one last gurgle it sank to the bottom. The other frog refused to give up. In the morning the farmer came out and found one live frog sitting on a big cake of butter.*

Frogs seem to get a lot of songs and stories made up about them. For instance, there's "Froggy Went a-Courting, "The Frog Prince," and my father's story, "The Foolish Frog." Maybe it's because frogs look a little bit like people. And maybe it's because we have something to learn from them. We certainly can learn some-

*thing from these two frogs who found themselves in an over-
whelming situation.*

*We live in an age of speed and convenience, after all.
Struggle? Don't waste your time. But once in a while the spend-
ing, not saving, of time and energy is the best thing for our minds
and bodies. Bake your own bread. Chop your own wood. Walk
your own body. Tell your own stories. And if you find yourself
lacking the confidence to take that first step, follow the example
offered by these stories: Renew something tried and true.*

3

Stories from Songs,
Rounds, and Lullabies

BEFORE THE WRITTEN word, storytellers told stories from memory. As a tale was retold and polished, retold and polished, details might be dropped, or facts might be fiddled with. Very often, storytellers used rhythm and rhyme to help them recall tales more precisely. The stories could be recited as a kind of poetry, chant, or even song.

I learned from my friend Ed Badeaux that many a song can be used to spin a tale. He made a story out of the old chain-gang chant, "Long John." But any camp song, nursery rhyme, or ballad can serve as a good starting point. This connection between story and song has always been strong. Although you don't need to be a musician to tell the stories in this section, music, in one way or another, is an important part of each of them.

I like to begin by asking the song a few questions. Why are three blind mice chasing the farmer's wife? Where, exactly, did Michael row his boat ashore? This is how "Abi-yoyo" came about. I never planned on retelling it in books and on records. I was just putting my kids to sleep by asking some questions of a traditional African lullaby.

In this day and age, I especially look for songs that show how people can come together to solve conflicts. Words can be slippery things and can sometimes keep people apart instead of bringing them together. But music has the power to leap language barriers. It bridges our differences and reaches the heart and mind in ways nearly impossible through words alone.

If there still is a human race here in a hundred years, I'm convinced that music will be one of the main reasons for our survival.

SAM THE WHALER

ONCE UPON A TIME, long ago, a boy lived on the banks of the Hudson River. He would look out of his window and watch the whaling ships, with their big white sails, sailing up the river, coming back from all around the world.

One evening he sat down to supper. "Ma," he said, "what's this? Mush for supper again?"

"Well, Sam," she said, "we don't have anything but mush. We can't afford chicken or expensive things like other people have."

Sam pushed his chair back from the table. "Ma," he said, "I'm tired of *mush* for breakfast, *mush* for lunch, *mush* for supper. I just don't feel like eating it anymore. I'm going out to find some work. And when I do, I'm going to buy you the best supper you've ever had." And he got up and walked out of the house. He walked down to the beautiful river where the beautiful boats were.

He listened to the sailors telling their stories. One of them was singing a song:

> *'Tis advertised in Boston, New York, and Buff-a-lo,*
>
> *One hundred brave Americans a-whaling for to go,*
>
> *Singing, Blow ye winds of the morning, so blow ye winds, hi! ho!*
>
> *Clear away your running gear and blow! blow! blow!*

Sam went over to an old sailor who sat on the dock whittling. "Is that true?" he asked. "Do they really want people to work on the boats and sail around the world catching whales?"

The sailor said, "Sure thing, son. If you want a job, just go over to the captain there."

Sam went over to the whaling boat and said, "Captain! Captain! You got a job for me? I'll shine the doorknobs! I'll scrub the decks! I'll do anything you want! I'll peel potatoes! I want to go with you! I want to sail around the world! I want to catch whales!"

"Well now, son," said the captain. "It's hard work. It doesn't pay very much."

"I still want to go! Please let me go with you!" begged Sam.

"Well, son, if you've got your mother's permission, it's all right with me. We need a cabin boy."

Sam ran home as fast as he could. "Ma! Ma! Pack my toothbrush! Pack an extra pair of pajamas! I've got a job! I'm going to sail around the world!"

"A job? Well, be careful, Sam. I'll miss you." His mother got together a little bag of all his precious things: his favorite cap, his penknife, his lucky rabbit's foot, and an extra comic book. And Sam ran back to the ship.

Up went the big sails! *Heave! Heave! Heave!* Then the captain yelled, "Now, haul up the anchor! We're sailing her down on the tide!"

Down the river they went, past Storm King, past Bear Mountain, down the river—Tarrytown! Yonkers! Spuyten Duyvil! And out on the open sea.

Sam looked around.

He looked to the east. Nothing but water.

He looked to the south. Nothing but water.

He looked in all directions. Nothing but water. They kept on sailing, the ship rocking from side to side.

After a few days at sea, the captain said, "Sam, climb up there in the crow's nest and look around. See if you can spot any whales."

"Crow's nest?" said Sam. "What's that?"

"See that little platform way up at the top of the mast? That's where you stand."

Sam went up—*pluck, plink, plink, pluck, pluck*—and held himself close against the mast. He had to hold on tight because when the wind blew, the mast bent *w-w-a-a-y* over to one side. He looked straight down, nothing but water. Then it bent *w-w-a-a-y* over to the other side. He looked straight down, nothing but water.

The captain hollered up, "Sam! Let loose of that mast! You've got to look for whales!"

So Sam did his best. He looked in all directions as the mast tipped back and forth. But all he saw was the blue sea. Until way off on the horizon, he thought he saw something. It looked like a fountain. *Pshew! Pshew! Pshew!*

"Thar she blows!" cried Sam.

And the captain hollered up, "Whar does she blow?!"

"Three points off the starboard bow!" answered Sam. And as quick as he could, he climbed down the mast.

Well, clear away the boats, m' boys, and after him we'll travel,

But if ye get too near his tail, he'll kick ye to the devil,

Singin': Blow ye winds of the mornin', blow ye winds Hi! Ho!

Clear away your runnin' gear and Blow! Blow! Blow!

The sailors jumped in the rowboat and they rowed and they rowed,

    and they rowed and they rowed,

       and they rowed.

They got nearer and nearer and nearer to the whale. They got so near they could almost touch it. They got very quiet. And the man with the harpoon drew back his hand...*s-w-a-p!* The whale thrashed. It dove deep. The rope attached to the harpoon was yanked out of the little boat. The whale surfaced and leaped into the air! *S-w-a-p!* went its tail against the side of the boat! It almost smashed them all up!

Finally, the whale tired. "Well, tow it alongside," said the mate, and the sailors pulled in on the rope.

Next comes the stowing down, m' boys,

t'will take both night and day,

And you'll all have fifty cents apiece

on the hundred and ninetieth day,

Singin': Blow ye winds of the mornin',

blow ye winds Hi! Ho!

Clear away your runnin' gear and Blow! Blow! Blow!

In the following months, Sam climbed up the mast many times. The mast swayed back and forth.

He'd look to the east. Nothing but water.

He'd look to the south. Nothing but water.

He'd look to the west. Nothing but water.

He'd look to the north. Nothing but water. Until one day, right up near a couple of icebergs, he saw it, *Pshew! Pshew! Pshew!*

"Thar she blows!" cried Sam.

And the captain hollered up, "Whar does she blow?!"

And Sam answered, "Five points off the port bow!" And down the mast he came, and into the rowboat they went. By now, Sam was allowed to join in the chase. They rowed as fast as they could. They rowed faster and they got nearer.

They got so near the whale they could almost touch it. And this time Sam was up in front. He had practiced with the harpoon so the captain let him be the one to throw it.

Sam drew back his hand. The harpoon was as sharp as a needle. The whole boat got very quiet. *S-w-a-p!* The whale thrashed. It dove deep. The rope attached to the harpoon was yanked out of the little boat. The whale surfaced and leaped into the air! *S-w-a-p!* went its tail against the side of the boat! It almost smashed them all up!

Finally, the whale tired. "Tow it alongside," said the mate, and the sailors pulled in on the rope.

Well, they caught long whales and short whales. Big whales and small whales. Spotted whales and striped whales and black whales and white whales.

Until finally, one day Sam and all the rest of the men said to the captain, "Captain, we're getting mighty tired of having nothing but *whale* stew and *whale* meat. *Whale* pancakes, *whale* salad, *whale* soup, *whale everything*! We want some nice fresh milk to drink and some nice green lettuce to eat."

The captain said, "Well now, don't you think we ought to get a couple more whales?"

"No," said the men. "It's time we turned around."

The captain asked, "Just one more?"

All the men stood together and said, "No, this is enough."
So right around they turned.

They sailed back across the ocean. Back in the direction from which they had come. A long time it took them, but one day they saw the hills. The hills of green, the hills of home. Into the Hudson River they sailed, past Spuyten Duyvil, past Yonkers, up the river—Tarrytown! Bear Mountain! Storm King! Until they could see a light way on top of Mount Beacon.

And Sam hollered to his friends, "There we are! We're home!"

The boat tied up at shore and the captain took out a big bag of silver dollars. Every man stood in line and took his turn. The captain paid out a handful of silver dollars to this man, a handful of silver dollars to that man. Finally, he came to Sam, the last one in line. The captain paid him one silver dollar.

Sam looked at his hand and said, "Holy mackerel! Is this all I get for working all this time?"

The captain said, "Well now, Sam, you were just learning, you know."

"Holy mackerel!" said Sam. And he called, "Hey, Joe! Hey, Pete! Look at all I got paid!"

The men came back and looked at Sam's one silver dollar. They said, "Hey now, look-a-here, Captain. If you want any of us to go out sailing with you again, you pay him just the same as us. He worked as hard as anybody else."

"Well," said the captain, "I suppose I've got to, if you all say so." And he took out his big bag of silver dollars and paid Sam one, two, three, four... a hundred silver dollars! The same as everybody else!

Sam ran up to town, straight to the grocery store, and he got himself the biggest box he could find. He filled it full of chicken and steaks and cakes and pies and potatoes and beans and peas and apples and all kinds of fruit.

He went home and his ma gave him a great big hug. "Sam! You're home!" And with the food he brought she fixed the biggest dinner they'd ever seen. She cooked this, she baked that, she boiled this. She piled it all on the table, and they both sat down. Sam ate and ate and ate, until he got so fat he could hardly touch the table. He ate until his stomach stuck out so far in front of him that he couldn't reach the table with his hands.

Then his ma gave him a little push off his chair and he rolled like a big marble across the floor. And she rolled him right into bed. She pulled the covers up to his chin, but he was so full, she couldn't tuck him in on the sides.

"Good night, Sam," she whispered. "Good night."

Sam went to sleep and dreamed he was out at sea. He was high up in the crow's nest, swaying from side to side. And way off in the distance he could see—*Pshew! Pshew! Pshew!* And he cried, "Thar she blows!"

Blow ye winds of the mornin', blow ye winds, Hi! Ho!

Clear away your runnin' gear and Blow! Blow! Blow!

Blow ye winds of the mornin', blow ye winds, Hi! Ho!

Clear away your runnin' gear and Blow! Blow! Blow!

"Sam the Whaler" is an unexpected favorite of my children and grandchildren. I wanted the boy in the story to be just on the threshold of getting big, even though an eleven-year-old wouldn't be strong enough to row a whaling boat. And, of course, his mother wouldn't let him go away so easily, either.

The tune is an old New Bedford whaling song from the early nineteenth century. I learned it back in 1939 when I was on Alan Lomax's radio show with a woman named Joanna Colcord. She'd been raised on her father's whaling ship and kept a little notebook of the songs sung by the sailors. Years later, she gathered them into a book called Songs of American Sailormen.

Alan asked me to learn one of them for the show—"New

Bedford Whalers." So I sat down and learned it on the spot. Fifteen years later, I made up the story to go with it. But I set the tale along the Hudson River instead of the coast of Massachusetts. Of course, today it's hard to imagine there ever was a whaling industry based along the Hudson. But in the early nineteenth century, there were whaling ships based in Hudson, Poughkeepsie, and Newburgh, to name just a few of the river towns.

The Whalers

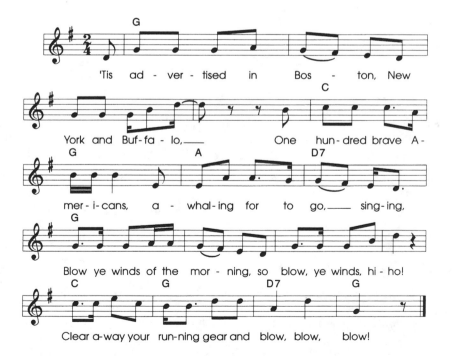

'Tis ad - ver - tised in Bos - ton, New York and Buf-fa - lo,____ One hun-dred brave A-mer - i- cans, a - whal-ing for to go,____ sing-ing, Blow ye winds of the mor - ning, so blow, ye winds, hi - ho! Clear a-way your run-ning gear and blow, blow, blow!

THE FALLS! THE FALLS!

IT WAS FIRST LIGHT and our twin-engine plane was flying over a wilderness, a thousand miles of forest. The navigator said to the engineer, "I think our radio's dead. I can hear, but I can't send. And it's bad weather ahead."

Then one of the engines began to sputter. The pilot said to the copilot, "The right engine's gone, but if we can make it over these mountains, I think I can set her down on that river below."

The plane barely cleared the peaks, and in the next valley quickly lost altitude. "Life jackets, everybody!" yelled the copilot. "We're gonna set her down on the river!" So five hundred miles from where we had radioed our last position, the pilot made an emergency belly-landing.

Twenty-five of us scrambled out of the escape hatch and

into the water. Twenty of us reached the shore just in time to turn and watch the great metal bird sink into the deep. "She'll rise no more," said the pilot. "Let us pray for the five we lost."

We splinted legs and arms, and bandaged wounds the best we could. Then we held a quick counsel. We had no food, no tools, no medicine. The navigator said, "There's got to be a town downriver." So we agreed to build a raft. The forest was so thick the river gave us the best chance for being spotted by rescuers.

We found some floating logs. We found some sharp stones. We cut some vines and made a raft. Have you ever tried to cut anything using only a sharp stone? It's not easy. We shaped long sticks into poles and paddles, and headed downstream.

Each of us did our best to work as a team. All except for this one guy who, even though he tried to help, just ended up in everyone's way. We called him "Book Boy," because all we'd ever seen him do was read. He wasn't able to paddle well or steer straight, but he kept trying to give us instructions, which we found pretty annoying. Every time we made some progress, he would tell us that a huge waterfall lay ahead.

"Where?" we all asked.

"I'm not sure," said Book Boy. "But I remember reading about it in a book."

"Well, I've never heard anything about a waterfall," said the navigator.

"And I didn't see anything from the air," said the pilot. "We have to keep this raft moving if we're going to find help."

What a nuisance Book Boy was! At the next sharp bend, the current picked up speed, and he yelled out, "The falls! The falls!"

"Where?" we yelled back.

"They're coming up," he insisted. "I'm sure of it. Pull ashore!" So we did as he said and sent out a scouting party.

But the party soon returned, their bodies tired and scratched. "The river is broad and smooth, as far as the eye can see," they said.

Once again, we boarded the raft and headed downstream, grumbling at Book Boy because of the hours we'd wasted. He just ignored us, and in his long-winded way kept on about the huge waterfall. He was so busy talking, he didn't even try to paddle.

"Be quiet, you give us all a pain," scolded the pilot. "Pitch in and do your part."

"But the falls! The falls!" cried Book Boy.

"Where?" shouted the navigator. "Just paddle!"

Around dusk, the river current again picked up speed as we rounded a sharp bend. And once again, because of Book Boy's talk, and his talk, and his talk, we pulled the raft ashore. If he hadn't spoken in such a self-confident and bookish tone, perhaps we wouldn't have listened at all. But now there was serious grumbling. The injured were getting worse. Every hour of delay endangered lives. And here we were, wasting a whole night on land.

At daylight, another scouting party set out. They soon returned. "The river is broad and smooth, as far as the eye can see," they said.

"We won't stop again!" the pilot yelled at Book Boy. "Grab a paddle and do something constructive."

"And if you won't paddle," added the navigator, "keep out of our way."

Once again, we boarded the raft and headed downstream.

But Book Boy kept insisting that the next bend in the river would reveal a huge waterfall. "That does it!" we told him, and we banished him to the back end of the raft. "Sit there and be quiet."

Now he sat at the stern while the rest of us faced forward, paddling with our aching arms and backs. Still, he didn't quit. He held on to the raft and leaned out over the water, trying to see around the next bend in the river. Then suddenly, Book Boy took out a sharp stone and began sawing and hacking apart the vines that bound together the stern. Up in front, we heard these sounds and turned to see Book Boy destroying the raft. "Stop!" we bellowed. "You'll drown us all!"

Book Boy didn't listen. He set to his task with even more determination. In a panic, and not knowing what else to do, the pilot swung his long pole. It knocked Book Boy overboard. But now the logs at the stern were starting to separate. The raft had become unbound! We paddled like mad for shore.

Once we reached safety, we didn't give another thought to Book Boy. We quickly set out to find more vines to tie the raft back together. A couple of men went downstream along the river. They soon returned, ashen faced. "It's the largest falls we've ever set eyes on! Just like Book Boy said. The whole river disappears over the edge and all you see is steam and spray rising from below. Not one of us would have survived! He saved us after all."

This story comes out of a song I wrote in 1969 called "All My Children of the Sun." The song has a fast-picking banjo accompaniment that underlines the suspense of the plot. The line, "All my children of the sun" serves as the refrain.

The story works as a kind of allegory and is probably best suited for a slightly older audience, perhaps sitting around a campfire. The weakness of any allegory, of course, is that it can become too pat. The meaning of a work of art can shift, change, expand. Today, the Book Boys of the world are still out there warning us about pollution, overpopulation, even catastrophic computer problems. Perhaps instead of seeing these Book Boys as nuisances, we should take the time to question our own assumptions.

All My Children of the Sun

1. The nav - i - ga - tor said to the en - gin - eer: "I

think our ra - di - o's dead.

I can hear,____ but I can't send, and

there's bad wea - ther a - head."____   The

pi - lot said to the co - pi - lot:

"Our right en - gine's gone.   But

if we can make it o - ver these moun - tains, per -

haps I can set her down."____   All   my

chil - dren of the sun.____

DICK WHITTINGTON
AND HIS CAT

WITH NO FAMILY to speak of and neighbors with little food or money to spare, young Dick Whittington was alone in the world. He did his best to find work. He asked at the village tavern. "Sorry, lad," said the tavern keeper. "A tavern's no place for a child."

He asked at the village stables. "Sorry, lad," said the stableman. "I've already got a stable boy."

He asked at the village blacksmith. "Sorry, lad," said the blacksmith. "I've got a wife and three children to feed." Dick started to walk away. "Wait a minute," called the blacksmith. "I can't send you off hungry. Sit here and share my lunch. I'll tell you a tale or two." And as they ate, the blacksmith told Dick stories about the magnificent city of London.

When they'd finished, Dick said, "I don't know how to thank you."

"Thank me?" said the blacksmith. "What kind of world is this, if two souls can't share a little food and story?"

"I guess you're right," said Dick. "I never thought of it that way. I won't forget it." And that very afternoon Dick set off for the city of London, filled with excitement and hope.

Now, can you imagine walking for days all by yourself toward a city where nobody knows you? Only to find a big, noisy place, that's dirty, too? It took all the courage Dick had. He did his best to find work in the city. He worked for pennies here and there, but he was so poor, he had to sleep in the street. Sometimes he woke up in the morning to find that his pennies had been picked from his pockets during the night!

Dick thought to himself, "I'll never get anywhere living like this." He decided that even his small village would be better than this hard city life.

He was sadly on his way back home when he spotted a cat limping down the road. Its paw was hurt and the animal looked nearly starved. Dick remembered the blacksmith's words: "What kind of world is this, if two souls can't share a little food and story?"

"Here kitty, kitty, kitty," called Dick. To his surprise, the cat limped over to him. Dick knelt down and used a piece of his shirt to gently wrap the cat's front paw. "There, kitty. That should help. Now, won't you share my lunch?" Dick had a crust of bread barely big enough to feed himself, but he broke it in two. "I'm just coming from London, and do I have stories to tell." And after eating the bread and listening to the stories, the cat followed Dick down the road.

The next morning Dick found a day's work with a farmer. He asked the farmer, "Could I get a little extra milk for my cat?"

"Sure," said the farmer. "A dairy farmer always has a little extra milk."

And after thanking the farmer, Dick Whittington and his cat left the farm and continued on their way. By now, the cat no longer limped and could catch its own food. And that afternoon, the cat caught not one, but two, field mice. "I see with a mended paw, you're a good mouser," said Dick.

Although they were far outside the city, Dick could still hear the bells of London. It seemed to him that the bells were saying:

> *Turn again, Whittington,*
> *Thou worthy citizen,*
> *Lord Mayor of London.*

"Lord Mayor of London?" said Dick, resting on a stone to listen. "Could I really be Lord Mayor of London? If I were, I could help people like me so they wouldn't have to sleep in the street." Then the bells again seemed to say:

Turn again, Whittington,

Thou worthy citizen,

Lord Mayor of London.

"Did you hear that, kitty?" said Dick. "Did I give up too easily? C'mon, we'll go back to London."

This time Dick headed straight for the city's waterfront. He didn't want to work on a ship. But he was a smart kid who watched everything. He had noticed businessmen buying shares in the profits of voyages. Dick wanted to buy shares and be a businessman, too, but shares cost money and he only had a few pennies. How would he ever become Lord Mayor of London?

One morning Dick got an idea. "I don't have gold or silver, but I do have something very valuable," he said to himself. And he asked one of the captains, "Do you ever have problems with mice on your ship?"

"Oh, quite often," said the captain. "There's one right now, climbing up the mooring line."

Dick nodded and told the captain, "You can't keep mice off a ship unless you have a good mouser."

"You're right," said the captain. "But a good one is hard to find."

"Well, I've got a great mouser. Hardest-working cat on the waterfront."

"And how much for this cat?" asked the captain.

"Nothing at all," said Dick.

"You mean, *free*?" asked the captain, looking at Dick suspiciously.

"Yes," said Dick. "If you agree to bring him back safe and sound, and give me a few shares in your voyage."

"Well," said the captain, laughing. "A fine mouser would be welcomed by my crew. And I'm sure your cat will be well fed. I'll put you down for a five-shilling share. It's not much, but you'll get a small piece of whatever comes in."

The next morning Dick said good-bye to his cat and watched the ship sail out of the harbor. Months and months passed. Dick managed to find odd jobs along the waterfront but made only a few pennies here and there. And he missed his cat very much.

Meanwhile, across the ocean . . .

The ship anchored in Morocco to trade with a king. The king had all the finest things in the world, but all his riches couldn't solve his biggest problem. His palace was overrun with mice.

"King, this is quite a problem you have," said the captain. "What would you give to be rid of these mice?"

Knowing this was impossible, the king rashly said, "Why, I'd give half my kingdom to be rid of them!"

The captain laughed, "First, see my solution." And he sent down to the ship for Dick's cat. In no time at all, the cat had cleared the mice from the palace. Then it jumped onto the king's lap and began to purr.

The king couldn't believe his eyes. "Such an animal!" he said. "Like a tiger to mice; like a dove to me. I must have it. Name your price."

"I'm sorry, I can't," said the captain. "It belongs to a poor boy in London. The cat is all he has."

"But I shall treat this cat like a king," said the king. "And as for the boy, he will never be poor again."

The captain thought of Dick sleeping in the street. "It is agreed then," said the captain. "But you must promise to take good care of the cat."

"That is a promise most easily made," said the king.

Now, even a small portion of the king's riches was an enormous amount of money. And when the captain returned to London, he found Dick still at work on the water-front, no closer to being a businessman.

"Greetings, Dick Whittington!" called the captain.

"Captain, you're back!" said Dick. He was busy sewing up holes in sacks of grain. "How was the voyage? How's my cat?"

"The voyage was wonderful," said the captain. "But I hope you won't be angry with me. I left your cat with somebody in even greater need of a mouser than myself. Your cat now lives in a palace with a king who promises to take good care of him."

"A palace? A king?"

"Yes, a king who values your cat above all else. And in appreciation he sent you these." The captain opened a chest filled with riches of every kind.

Dick's eyes had never seen such jewels and gold. He picked up a few of the coins and stared at them. But his amazement soon fell to sadness. "These mean nothing if my cat is not well cared for."

"He's being cared for like a king," assured the captain.

Dick didn't know whether to be angry or overjoyed. But just then, a ragged boy and girl came up to him and asked, "Could you spare a penny, friend, if we helped you sew those sacks?"

Dick looked at the captain. Then he looked at the two children no different than himself. Once again, he remembered the blacksmith's words.

"You both look hungry and tired," said Dick. "Come, let me buy you a meal and find you proper lodging. I have such stories to tell."

"Are you teasing?" said the little girl.

"Of course not," said Dick. "What kind of world is this, if three souls can't share a little food and story?"

"Dick Whittington" is a true story, which I've loosely retold with a few fanciful additions. The real Dick Whittington lived in England about six hundred years ago and was Lord Mayor of London, not once, but three times. He was also a major benefactor to the poor and a pioneer in the world of philanthropy—not a small feat, considering the time. I first learned "Dick Whittington" as a song, not as a story. We sang it in school. It's a short song that makes a lovely round when sung by three people. A teacher of mine said there was a story behind the song, but I learned only the bare bones: A poor boy goes to London to seek his fortune; along the way he befriends a cat.

Over the years, I used this simple framework for my own retelling. It was only while putting this book together that I saw written versions of the story. In all of them, it's a rich family that provides Whittington with a roof over his head and owns the ship that takes his cat overseas. And it's the daughter of this family that befriends Whittington and eventually marries him, but only after he becomes rich.

I'm not sure I like that story line. Are rich friends the only route to worthy citizenship? I don't want to stress that as a lesson for children. I prefer to stress Whittington's own generosity and ingenuity and the belief that sharing a little food and story (or song) goes a long way toward improving human relationships.

Turn   Again,   Whittington

CUMBERLAND MOUNTAIN
BEAR CHASE

Away, away, we're bound for the mountain,
Bound for the mountain, bound for the mountain,
Over the hills, the fields, and the fountain
Away to the chase, away.

Rover, Rover, see him, see him,
Rover, Rover, catch him, catch him,
Over the mountain, the fields, and the fountain
Away to the chase, away!

ONCE THERE WAS a little boy who wanted to go out bear hunting with his father. But his father would always say, as fathers do, "No, you're too young. Stay at home."

While the father was out all night with the hounds, the boy was supposed to be asleep. But he'd lie in bed, listening. He'd hear the hounds baying far off in the distance and could tell by their barks whether they were on the bear's trail or off the trail, or if they finally had a bear treed. The boy wished he was out there, too.

In the morning, the boy would beg and beg his father to let him go out hunting. "C'mon, Pa, I won't be a bother. I won't slow you down. Please, please, let me come with you."

He got to be such a pest that one day his father said, "All right, all right, you can come with me . . . , but on your next birthday. Not today."

Now, the boy's next birthday was many, many months away, but he didn't forget. And when it finally rolled around, as birthdays always do, he reminded his father of the promise. "It's my birthday. I can come hunting with you."

"Well," the father said, "I reckon I did say something like that. All right. You can come with me. But don't expect me to slow down. If you get lost out in those woods, just remember to keep going downhill. Sooner or later you'll find the road."

The boy was too excited to be frightened. "That's all right," he thought to himself. "I'll take my horn along. If I get lost, I'll blow it. Old Blue, he'll hear me. He'll find me and bring me home." Old Blue was the lead hound dog and the boy's favorite.

Night rolled around and off they went. The boy had his horn strung over his shoulder and, in his pocket, a few cookies and his lucky penny.

But, you know, the boy couldn't keep up. He tried his best, but the hounds went faster and faster. His father went faster and faster. And the boy got farther and farther behind, his horn swinging from one side to the other.

Before the boy knew it, he was out in the woods all by himself. And it was *dark*. He had never been alone in the woods at night.

He ate one of his cookies and swallowed every last crumb. He rubbed his lucky penny. Then he took hold of his horn and trumpeted a call.

Old Bluuuue, where are youuuuu?

All he heard was a hoot owl.

Hoo-hoo, hoo-hoo.

The boy listened and listened. No sign of the hounds.

He ate the other cookie and swallowed every last crumb. He rubbed his lucky penny. Then he blew the horn again.

Old Bluuuuuue, where are youuuuu?

But all he heard was the hoot owl.

Hoo-hoo, hoo-hoo.

Then—suddenly, way off in the distance, he could hear...
ow..., *ow*..., **ow**..., **ow**... The sound of the hound dogs
got louder and louder.

"I hear them!" the boy yelled. "I knew Old Blue would
come back. And here they come, right around the mountain. Right to where I am!"

> *Listen to the hound dog's heavy bay,*
>
> *Sounding high over the way.*
>
> *All night long till the break of dawn,*
>
> *Merrily the chase goes on.*
>
> *Over the mountain, the hills, and the fountain*
>
> *Away to the chase, away!*

"Listen to Old Blue getting on the bear's trail!" called the
boy. "Sounds like Bugle Boy's got the trail, too. Smart old
dog, that Bugle Boy! And there's Crickety, right along with
them."

Then the boy saw his father running past. He realized
he'd been very close to that bear when he'd blown his horn

to call Old Blue! The boy shouted to his father, "I think they've got that bear treed now. Listen to 'em bay!"

Ow ow ow ow ow!

"I think you're right," the father shouted back. "And it was your call that turned them in the right direction. You can come hunting with us anytime."

"You mean that, Pa?" asked the boy.

"Sure I do," said the father. "Let's go!"

Away, way, we're bound for the mountain,

Bound for the mountain, bound for the mountain,

Over the hills, the fields, and the fountain

Away to the chase, away!

In the 1930s, this song appeared on a 78 rpm record by the Tennessee banjo picker, Uncle Dave Macon. It was called "The Cumberland Mountain Deer Race." In the 1940s, Alan Lomax changed it to "The Cumberland Mountain Bear Chase" for a radio show. I was on a one-week furlough from the army, and Woody Guthrie, Lee Hays, Cisco Houston, and I helped provide music for that show. In the 1950s, I made up the accompanying

*story for my kids, and in the 1990s, my coauthor, Paul, added
still more. The folk process moves forward.*

*The song has an exciting, fast-paced melody that really gives
the feel of a chase. If you don't play an instrument, try reciting
the chorus as quickly and rhythmically as you can to give it that
galloping feel. Or why not try rewriting the lyrics to fit your own
situation? The story can be about anything kids want to do before
their parents think they're old enough—pouring their own juice,
crossing the street, riding a bike:*

Away, way, we're bound for the bike path,

Bound for the bike path, bound for the bike path,

Over the streets, to the park, and the bike path

Away to the ride, away!

Cumberland Mountain Bear Chase

A - way, a - way, we're   bound for the moun - tain,

bound   for the moun - tain,   bound   for the moun - tain,

O - ver the hills,   the   fields   and the foun - tain,   a -

way   to the chase,   a - way,   a - way.

Ro - ver,   Ro - ver,   see   him,   see   him,
Lis - ten   to the hound dog's   hea - vy   bay,___

Ro - ver,   Ro - ver, catch him,   catch him.   All night long till the
sound - ing high___   o - ver the way.   _

break   of   dawn   mer - ri - ly   the   chase goes on.

O - ver the hills,   the   fields   and the foun - tain,   a -

way   to the chase,   a - way,   a - way!

A B I Y O Y O

ONCE UPON A TIME, there was a little boy who played the ukulele. He'd go around town, **plink!** *plonk! plonk!* **plink! plink!** *plonk!*

"Take that thing out of here!" the grown-ups would tell him.

Not only that. The boy's father got in trouble, too.

His father was a magician. He had a magic wand. He could go *Zoop!* and make things disappear. But he played too many tricks on people.

He'd come up to someone doing a hard job of work like sawing wood, *zz-zzt, zz-zzt.*

Zoop! The saw disappears.

He'd come up to someone about to drink a nice cold glass of something.

Zoop! The glass disappears.

He'd come up to someone about to sit down after a hard day's work.

Zoop! No chair.

People got tired of this. They said to the father, "You get out of here. Take your magic wand and your practical jokes, and you and your son just git."

The boy and his father were *ostracized.* That means, the villagers made them live way out on the edge of town.

Now, in this town they used to tell stories. The old people used to tell stories about the giants that lived in the old days. They used to tell a story about a giant called Abiyoyo. They said he was as tall as a tree and could eat... **people...up!** Of course, nobody believed the story, but they told it anyway.

One day, one day, the sun rose blood red over the hills. The first people got up and looked out the window. They saw a great big shadow in front of the sun. They could feel the whole ground shake.

Women screamed. "*Eeekkk!*" Strong men fainted. "*Ohhh...*"

"Run for your lives! Abiyoyo is coming!"

Down through the fields he came. He came to the sheep

pasture. He grabbed a whole sheep. *Yeowp!* He ate it down in one bite.

He came to the cow pasture and grabbed a whole cow. *Yuhk!*

People yelled, "Grab your most precious possessions and run! Run!...R U N !"

Just then, way over on the edge of town, the boy and his father woke up. The boy rubbed his eyes. "Hey, Pa, what's coming over the fields?"

"Oh, son, it's Abiyoyo! Oh, if only I could get him to lie down, I could make him disappear!"

The boy said, "Come with me, Father!" He grabbed his father by one hand. The father grabbed the magic wand. The boy grabbed his ukulele. Over the fields they ran. Right up to Abiyoyo.

People screamed, "Don't go near him! He'll eat you alive!"

There was Abiyoyo! He had long fingernails 'cause he never cut 'em...Slobbery teeth 'cause he never brushed 'em...Stinking feet 'cause he never washed 'em.

He raised up his big claws and...

Just then, the boy whipped out his ukulele and began to sing:

A-bi-yo-yo, A-bi-yo-yo

A-bi-yo-yo, A-bi-yo-yo

A-bi-yo-yo, yo yoyo, yo yoyo

A-bi-yo-yo, yo yoyo, yo yoyo

Well, you know, the giant had never heard a song about himself before. A foolish grin spread over his face. The giant started to dance. Kicked up his heels.

A-BI-YO-YO, A-BI-YO-YO

The boy went faster.

A-BI-YO-YO, YO YOYO, YO YOYO

A-BI-YO-YO, YO YOYO, YO YOYO

The giant got out of breath. He staggered. He fell down flat on the ground.

Up stepped the father with his magic wand. ***Zoop! Zoop!***

People looked out their windows. "Abiyoyo's disappeared! He's gone!" They ran across the fields. They lifted the boy and his father up on their shoulders. "Come back to

town. Bring your darn ukulele. We don't care anymore."
And they all sang:

> *A-bi-yo-yo, A-bi-yo-yo*
>
> *A-bi-yo-yo, A-bi-yo-yo*
>
> *A-bi-yo-yo, yo yoyo, yo yoyo*
>
> *A-bi-yo-yo, yo yoyo, yo yoyo*

So ever since that day in that little town, whenever parents put their children to sleep, they tell the story about the giant named Abiyoyo.

And it *is* a good story to go to sleep on.

> *A-bi-yo-yo, A-bi-yo-yo*
>
> *A-bi-yo-yo, A-bi-yo-yo*
>
> *A-bi-yo-yo, yo yoyo, yo yoyo*
>
> *A-bi-yo-yo, yo yoyo, yo yoyo*

Back in 1952, I was given a book called African Folk Songs *notated by J. N. Maselwa and Rev. H. C. N. Williams. A small footnote appeared beneath the song "Abiyoyo":*

This is a lullaby. It comes at the conclusion of a bedtime story in which a monster figures as someone who threatens little children. The children are given a charm for their protection, which inspires them to sing this song, the rhythm of which affects the monster so powerfully that he is induced to dance. In this state of emotion he is quickly dispensed with by the fathers and mothers of the children. The song is sung until the babe is asleep.

From this brief description, I first improvised this story for my own children.

The funny thing about improvising is that you don't always know how things are going to turn out. When I began "Abiyoyo," I only knew that I wanted to end with the giant's defeat. But I'm kind of a pacifist, so I didn't want the story to end with a sword. I asked myself, "Why couldn't it be done with music?" I've believed in the power of music all my life. Of course, a little magic also helps.

Even without my urging, people have made up different versions of "Abiyoyo." One told by some camp counselors on Fire Island was unique. They called their giant Babi-Abi and had him rising out of the water.

As with any story in this book, but especially "Abiyoyo," I encourage you to use sounds, motions—anything to help make the

tale come alive. When the boy and his father are ostracized I always point my finger away and make a kicking motion. Or when
Abiyoyo appears over the hills, I use an ominous, shaking voice
and make a stomping noise with my feet. Then I hold my arms
outstretched and curl my fingers like claws. Don't be afraid to
dance and sing the lullaby or even fall down on the floor exhausted. That way, you'll be ready for bedtime, too. And if you
still have any energy left, string the chorus out for a good, long
time, gradually singing it more and more softly until someone
falls asleep.

A b i y o y o

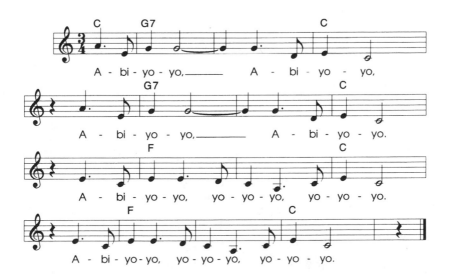

ABIYOYO RETURNS

THIRTY YEARS LATER . . .

A little girl played her drum as she marched around town. *Poom-i-ty, poom-poom; poom-i-ty, poom-poom.* She and her parents were the town musicians. Her father played the ukulele and her mother played the flute. Together, the three of them made up a little band. If there was a wedding or a birthday party or a parade, the little girl and her parents were sure to be invited.

Now, over the years, this town had grown a little too quickly. The townspeople had chopped down more and more trees to make way for more houses and more farms. The valley that was once covered by forests was now stripped bare.

Did you know that forests are important? The soil is

dense with the roots of the trees and it acts like a big sponge. It absorbs rainwater and holds it until the next dry spell. But without any trees, the soil can't hold moisture. The rain runs right off the fields. So each and every spring this town had floods. And each and every summer this town had droughts.

Something had to be done.

The townspeople put their heads together. "If we build a small dam," they said, "we could catch the spring floods and save the water to irrigate the fields in summer." Of course, they shouldn't have chopped down so many trees in the first place. But they didn't know that.

After careful planning, the town started to build the dam. This was long ago before people had bulldozers and tractors. All the work had to be done with picks and shovels. Everybody had to pitch in and dig, dig, dig.

But guess what happened? They struck an *enormous* boulder! At first, the townspeople thought they could dig around it. But the more dirt they removed, the more rock they uncovered. It was as big as a house! And no one had any idea how to move it. They tried pulleys and levers and winches. Nothing worked.

Now, in this town they still told stories about the giants

that lived in the old days. And one of these stories was about the giant called Abiyoyo. He was as tall as a tree and could eat people up. But the little girl who played the drum knew that long ago her father and grandfather had saved the town by making Abiyoyo disappear. Why couldn't they do it again?

"Daddy," she said, "I bet Abiyoyo could move that rock."

Her father laughed and said, "I suppose he could."

"Then why not bring him back?" said the little girl. "Grandpa still has his magic wand. Once the rock is moved, Grandpa can go *Zoop! Zoop!* and make Abiyoyo disappear again."

"Bring back Abiyoyo?" asked her mother. "Are we talking about the same angry giant that eats people up?"

"But if we make him lots of good food, he won't eat us," said the little girl. "And if we sing him lots of good songs, he won't get mad at us."

"Songs?" laughed her father. "That might not work this time."

"And what if we run out of good things for him to eat?" said her mother. "What then?"

"But if we don't bring back Abiyoyo," pleaded the little girl, "we'll never get the dam built."

"Leave that to grown-ups," said her parents. "Now, no more talk of Abiyoyo."

But none of the grown-ups knew what to do. Days and weeks passed and the boulder stayed right where it was. No one could work on the dam. Finally, the little girl's father said, "It looks like Abiyoyo is our only hope."

That afternoon the family went to see Grandpa. "Bring back Abiyoyo?" he exclaimed. "A hungry giant is very dangerous."

"But no one else can move the rock," said the little girl.

"Hmmm," said Grandpa. "I see your point." He opened his old trunk of magic things and pulled out capes, colored scarves, a crumpled top hat, a rubber chicken. "Oh, here it is," he said, blowing dust off the magic wand. "Shall we see if it still works?"

And with a *Zoop!* the little girl's drum suddenly disappeared. "Hey, Grandpa, give that back," she said.

And with a *Zoop!* the drum reappeared. "I guess I still have the magic touch," Grandpa said with a giggle.

Over the next few days everybody in the town cooked their best recipes and practiced their best songs. Finally, they were ready. Grandpa built a special fire out of special wood that made a special kind of smoke. Then he waved his special wand in a special way and recited the special magic words. A few seconds passed, then...

Zooooooop!

Just like that, there was Abiyoyo standing even bigger than before. Bigger than a tall tree. Standing there with his long fingernails and slobbery teeth and stinking feet.

Women screamed. *"Eeekkk!"* Strong men fainted. *"Ohhh...* Abiyoyo's returned!"

"Quiet," shushed the little girl. "You'll make him angry."

Abiyoyo looked sleepy and scruffy. He needed a shave and was covered in cobwebs. He gave a big yawn and a big stretch. "OHHHH," he bellowed. "I'M HUNGRY!"

But the townspeople were well prepared. Arranged on tables were platters of pasta and chicken and meat loaf and salad and fresh fruit, and all sorts of good things to eat.

Yeowp! Abiyoyo ate a whole pot of stew in one gulp.

Yuhk! Abiyoyo ate a whole loaf of bread in one bite.

Yeowp! Yeowp! Abiyoyo ate a whole roast beef in two gulps.

Yuhk! Yuhk! Abiyoyo ate a whole cake and a whole pudding in two bites. "I feel better already," he said, rubbing his tummy.

"Abiyoyo, are you still strong?" asked the little girl.

"OF COURSE!" Abiyoyo said.

"Really?" said the little girl. "Strong enough to lift that huge boulder?"

"HUMPH, I FEEL STRONG ENOUGH TO LIFT ANY-THING," said Abiyoyo.

"I don't believe you," said the little girl. "Prove it."

Abiyoyo leaned down, picked up the enormous boulder, and threw it high in the air. Up it went. Higher. Higher! HIGHER! It sailed in a big arc, then landed *KER-RUMPH!* Dirt flew in all directions. The whole town cheered, "Hooray for Abiyoyo!" People hugged each other. Boys and girls danced. Dogs barked for joy.

"I'M HUNGRY!" bellowed Abiyoyo.

But the food was all eaten up. The little girl saw her chance and began to play her drum. *Poom-i-ty poom-poom; poom-i-t-y, poom-poom,* it rang out as she marched around Abiyoyo's feet. Her father tuned up his ukulele and he began to play, too, *Plink-plink, plink-plink.* Then her mother joined in on her flute, *Toot-toot, toot-toot.* And everybody began to sing:

A-bi-yo-yo, A-bi-yo-yo

A-bi-yo-yo, A-bi-yo-yo

A-bi-yo-yo, yo yoyo, yo yoyo

A-bi-yo-yo, yo yoyo, yo yoyo

And, you know, a foolish grin spread over Abiyoyo's face. "HEY, IT'S MY SONG!" he yelled with excitement. He forgot all about eating, and started to dance and sing.

A-BI-YO-YO, A-BI-YO-YO

A-BI-YO-YO, A-BI-YO-YO

His big feet shook the ground. He accidentally stepped on a table. CRASH went the table. "Oops," said Abiyoyo. Mothers and fathers rushed to take their children out of the way. The little girl and her parents played faster.

A-BI-YO-YO, YO YOYO, YO YOYO

A-BI-YO-YO, YO YOYO, YO YOYO

And faster. And faster, until the giant got so out of breath, he fell down flat on the ground. "OOOHHH," Abiyoyo groaned. "I HAVEN'T DANCED IN SUCH A LONG TIME."

And the next thing you know, he closed his eyes and snored the loudest snores you ever heard. They rumbled like thunder. *ZZZZZZTTTT! BLUBBBB-BLUBB-BBBBB...*

"Now's our chance!" said the little girl. "But where's Grandpa? He's supposed to be here with his magic wand."

"Last I saw," said her mother, "he was right over there." They all looked over to where she was pointing. But all they saw was the boulder.

"Oh no!" shrieked the little girl. "Grandpa!"

They heard a little groan. "Ohhhh." They all ran over.

"Grandpa, are you all right?" asked the little girl.

"I'm OK, I think," said Grandpa. "A little shaken up. The boulder just missed me."

"But where's your magic wand?" the little girl whispered.

"I'm not sure. When the boulder hit, I must have dropped it."

"It's over here," said the little girl's father, picking up a handful of tiny pieces.

Everybody looked at the sleeping giant. Then at the broken wand. Then at the little girl. "You got us into this," the townspeople said. "How are you going to get us out of it?"

"Haven't we learned anything?" asked the little girl. "As long as Abiyoyo has lots of good food he won't eat us. And as long as we sing him lots of good songs, he won't get mad at us."

"It might just work," said Grandpa.

"I've always believed in the power of good music," said her mother.

"And I've always believed in the power of good food," said her father.

Believe it or not, the little town learned to live with its giant. And it wasn't long before Abiyoyo's anger seemed to disappear. He got so fond of the little girl and her parents, they became like a family. Abiyoyo slept in the barn with his feet sticking out the double doors. And he learned to brush his teeth and wash his feet.

And the townspeople? Well, they built their small dam and planted a lot of new trees on the hillsides. And most importantly, they never forgot how to share good food and they never forgot how to share good songs.

A-bi-yo-yo, A-bi-yo-yo,

A-bi-yo-yo, A-bi-yo-yo,

A-bi-yo-yo, yo yoyo, yo yoyo

A-bi-yo-yo, yo yoyo, yo yoyo

I made up this story for Lee Hays, who told me, "Pete, you have to have a sequel. Poor Abiyoyo! You can't just leave him out in limbo."

Over the years I've attempted different versions, but none was very successful. The basic idea wasn't bad. The little boy is all grown up. He has a daughter of his own. Their little town lives at peace and grows and grows but discovers that a town can't grow forever. In the long run, every community must learn to manage its giants, whoever, and whatever, they might be.

By the way, for those of you who are real sticklers for stories that make sense, you might be wondering why Grandpa couldn't just Zoop! Zoop! the huge boulder away. Well, I took it upon myself to put this question to Grandpa directly. Here's his answer: "My wand doesn't work on rocks. It's a rule of magic. Otherwise, I could make the whole earth disappear. And that's too much power for any one person to hold."

Too bad Grandpa's rule only exists in stories. It's a good rule to have.

Abiyoyo

A - bi - yo - yo,_____ A - bi - yo - yo,

A - bi - yo - yo,_____ A - bi - yo - yo.

A - bi - yo - yo, yo - yo - yo, yo - yo - yo.

A - bi - yo - yo, yo - yo - yo, yo - yo - yo.

4 Some Stories from America's History

*T*HE HISTORY OF the United States is a long, varied, and complicated story made up of countless small stories that I've learned—and you've learned, too—from books, articles, anecdotes, and songs. I retell some of these stories, both onstage and at home, filling in where memory fails me, adding a scene here, a little dialogue there. My story's not exactly the way it happened, but it might have happened this way.

I particularly enjoy telling anecdotes that show why something succeeded; how people with all the strikes against them still managed to make a situation work. I tell these stories hoping that other people, especially young people, might learn by example.

Too often our knowledge of history goes no farther than a name or a date. We establish holidays, build memorials, and name public works to commemorate important figures and events. But soon we forget. Presidents' Day comes to mean a day off from school, the Fourth of July means fireworks, and the Statue of Liberty means sightseeing.

But when kids get to be eight or ten years old, they start taking an interest in the bigger world around them and its history—how things got this way. I've included a few of these stories in this book. Some others might be: How did Harriet Tubman lead slaves along the Underground Railroad? Why were the Wright brothers successful inventors? What became of Geronimo and his people? Discovering the true stories behind legendary figures can be exciting.

It's up to each of us to tell the stories that make history come alive again. In Fishkill, New York, they read the Declaration of Independence on the Fourth of July, and in schools and churches all across America, the "I Have a Dream" speech is read on Martin Luther King Day.

That said, remember that history is not limited to tales of "great" people and important events. In fact, it's mostly made up of the stories of people who simply lived their lives. How did your uncle win the Purple Heart? What was your town like before the interstate came through? When did your mother open her first restaurant?

There are also family adventures, like my father's story, "The Trailer and the Flood." And still other adventures that I call "across-the-ocean" stories. How did your grandmother travel from Hungary to America? Where in China did your great-aunt come from? Why did your father emigrate from Ghana?

The very questions that help reporters write news stories can just as easily evoke a family story. What happened? Who did it happen to? Where did it happen? When, why, and how? With a little snooping around, you might discover something unexpected or inspirational. And whether sad, serious, or funny, these family tales make up who we are. They're our personal history. It's crucial to retell these small stories, these small victories.

The twenty-first century is upon us. What kinds of stories are we going to tell? My guess is we'll tell about new dangers and new hopes. But how can we know where we're heading if we don't know where we've been?

KING OF AMERICA?

HALF HIDDEN AMONG the trees in Newburgh, New York, sits an old Dutch farmhouse made of fieldstone. George Washington lived in this house when he turned down the chance to become the King of America. It's a true story. You've never heard it?

The American Revolution was over and the Americans had won the war. The British general, Cornwallis, defeated at Yorktown, had sailed back to England with all his troops. But because a peace treaty still hadn't been signed, some English ships remained in New York City's harbor. For a whole year an American delegation in Paris, led by Benjamin Franklin, argued with British officials over the terms of the treaty.

Back in Newburgh, sixty miles north of New York City, General Washington felt it wise to keep the American army together in case war should break out again. It wasn't a large force, just a few thousand soldiers camped out in log cabins in the little town of New Windsor, a stone's throw away from Newburgh. During this time, the spring of 1782, Washington might have written a letter such as this to his wife:

My Dear Martha,

I write this to you as I look out over the Hudson River. The view is spectacular.

Two miles south, three thousand of our troops are building log huts to live in. We don't know how long we'll be here—a few months, a year, or more. Word comes from our commissioners in Paris that the King's representatives continue to delay the signing of a peace treaty.

Of you, I have a request. I ask that you join me here in New York. I've taken up residence in an old Dutch farmhouse, and as I said, the view is stunning. More beautiful than anything we can boast of along the Potomac.

I realize this request requires a long and arduous

journey—two weeks if by coach and still longer if by
sea—but I hope you will consider it.

Your loving husband,

George

As we now know, Martha did join George Washington at
Newburgh, and it so suited her that she stayed for a whole
year.

Meanwhile in Philadelphia, America's struggling new
government, the Continental Congress, commanded very
little power. Taxes went uncollected and the paper money
issued by Congress couldn't buy anything. The phrase went
around the country that if something had no value, it was
"not worth a Continental."

Washington's officers grew increasingly frustrated with
the new government. The money that should have paid
their salaries—and the salaries of their troops—was worth-
less and it seemed that Congress might never gain the
power necessary to run the country. The officers complained, "The government calls this pay? They give us this
Continental script that's not worth the paper it's printed on.
Few merchants will accept it, and how can we blame them?

Somebody has to take control, and who better than our General Washington?"

Eventually, the officers presented Washington with a letter:

> *General,*
>
> *You must take over the reins of government. We need a voice of authority, not a bickering crowd. The Continental Congress is useless. It's allowing the country to fall to pieces. We will follow wherever you lead.*

Washington sent for one of his colonels. "Colonel, go out and get every officer who signed this letter. They deserve an answer in person. I'll address them outside the house at nine o'clock tomorrow morning."

The next morning arrived, and Washington, before giving his reply, searched for his eyeglasses, a relatively new invention. "Having grown gray in the service of my country," he said, "it seems I am now growing blind."

The officers awaited his answer with bated breath.

Still, Washington delayed, looking at each officer in turn. Finally he spoke.

"I am surprised you do not share my republican convictions. I did not spend six years fighting royalty to set up a new royalty. I did not defeat the King to become a king myself. I do not want to hear of such a suggestion again."

He dismissed the officers. He had passed up the only chance anyone's ever had to become King of America.

⟵⟶

Following the American Revolution, Washington could easily have taken over the government. But Washington was more dedicated to America's fledgling democracy than to making himself a king. This is why he was so loved. "First in war, first in peace, first in the hearts of his countrymen." How many times in history has a general overthrown the establishment and then refused to assume absolute power? Only in a few cases.

Washington's officers compared him to one such general from Roman days, General Cincinnatus. After successfully leading the Roman troops to victory, Cincinnatus refused to return to Rome and become one of its consuls. Instead, he went back to his farm. "I have helped save Rome, now I am going back to my old life," he said. This is the historical ideal of the citizen soldier.

But as inspiring as Washington's example is, I tell this story mostly because my wife, Toshi, and I can see the landmark from our window. The surrounding landscape has changed, of course. There's a yellow smokestack on that edge of the Hudson now, and a big junkyard, too. Yet, we can look out across the river at the city of Newburgh and see the old Dutch farmhouse made of field-stone. It's something our children and grandchildren have grown up with. It's part of our history and part of our country's history.

You don't have to look far to discover such stories in your neighborhood. There are any number of historic landmarks in and around most cities and towns. There are historic markers dotting roadsides and highways. And don't forget about your local historical society or public library, both of which are fine story resources.

THE EMANCIPATION
PROCLAMATION

HISTORY BOOKS TELL us that Abraham Lincoln freed the slaves, but he's only one hero in the story. The rest are ordinary American citizens like you and me.

For two hundred years, there were only a few people who said slavery was a bad thing. In the 1830s, these folks organized themselves into what was called the abolitionist movement. Abolitionists aimed to abolish slavery in the United States, although a majority of the country disagreed with them.

One man, Elijah Lovejoy, in the state of Illinois, published an abolitionist newspaper. People told Elijah, "Oh, you're one of those crazy people who wants to change the world."

Some people believed so strongly in slavery that they threatened Elijah. "Keep printing that paper and we'll make you wish you hadn't," they told him.

"I'm entitled to my opinion," he said. "And I'll stand up for what I think is right."

Well, these proslavery people didn't like Elijah Lovejoy's reply at all. So they destroyed his printing press and burned down his newspaper office. This happened several times.

But Elijah Lovejoy didn't give up. He passed the hat among his friends and raised enough money to buy another printing press. It came all the way from Boston and took a month or more to arrive. Folks back then didn't have planes and big tractor trailers to deliver things quickly like we do today. In the meantime, Elijah set up a new office.

After the new press arrived, a mob of proslavery people surrounded his office and said, "Elijah Lovejoy, we're going to burn down your building."

Elijah Lovejoy refused to move. "Over my dead body," he said.

They shot him. They destroyed his press again.

Now, Elijah Lovejoy wasn't the only member of his family who was against slavery. He had a younger brother named Owen who was a pastor as well as an abolitionist.

And some twenty years after Elijah was killed, Owen became a congressman. A few years after that, Abraham Lincoln was elected president.

As the country's leader, Lincoln had to make a difficult decision whether or not to sign the piece of paper on his desk called the Emancipation Proclamation. The proclamation would abolish slavery in all areas controlled by the U.S. Army. But while some people thought it was the fair thing to do, others were steadfast against it, saying it would destroy the nation's economy. Owen Lovejoy, in the spirit of his brother, wrote Lincoln a letter: "Mr. President, I think your heart is in the right place. Why don't you sign the Emancipation Proclamation?"

What President Lincoln wrote back was very interesting. He said, in effect, "I can't sign the Emancipation Proclamation right yet. But you keep on pushing." In other words, Lincoln needed pressure to come from the public before he could sign controversial legislation like the Emancipation Proclamation. So Lovejoy and others continued to write letters and hold meetings to spread the abolitionists' message.

Not long after, the Emancipation Proclamation was signed. It didn't get signed just because Lincoln picked up his pen and signed it. It got signed because ordinary people like you and me pushed forward and made their voices heard.

———

When telling these stories, I often take a little creative license. I want to weave a good tale as much as give a good history lesson. So if I need dialogue, I make it up. Or if I need to fast-forward twenty years through Owen Lovejoy's life, I do.

Too often we think of the past as fixed and closed and separate from our lives. But history doesn't come ready-made in a book. It's what happens to ordinary people through time and circumstance. Events back then are as connected to events right now as people back then are connected to people right now.

Chances are you could uncover some of these connections. I had a great-grandfather named Edwin Seeger who was a horse-and-buggy doctor in Massachusetts. He was also an abolitionist. And for many African Americans, Lincoln's Emancipation Proclamation meant freedom for their ancestors. These connections help to remind us that we are participants in the story, not simply bystanders.

THE PREACHER'S
FALSE TOOTH

LONG AGO THERE was a preacher named Hays who traveled from town to town, mostly on horseback, preaching here and preaching there. He was in charge of a number of churches, spread out over a large area in the state of Arkansas. At each stop someone from the local congregation would put him up for the night. He'd get simple accommodations: a bed, clean sheets, and a meal or two.

On one particular Saturday, the preacher's hosts were a farmer and his wife. The couple waved to the preacher as he came up the road, dust rising behind him. *Clip clop. Clip clop.* An old horse only goes so fast. The farmer helped the preacher down. They put the horse in the barn. Then the farmer and the preacher walked through the yard where some chickens roamed freely, pecking here and there. They went into the house and sat down to an evening meal that consisted of little but potatoes and bread.

After Saturday supper, the preacher excused himself and retired to his room to prepare Sunday's sermon. He worked for a bit, then got ready for bed. But this preacher couldn't simply brush his teeth before going to sleep. He had a false tooth that he took out each night to clean. He carefully unscrewed the tooth, washed it, and placed it on the windowsill to dry for the night. Then the preacher went back to put the finishing touches on his sermon before he went to bed.

But when he awoke in the morning, the tooth had disappeared. "Where could it have gone to?" he asked himself. He looked on the floor and underneath the bed. He checked his mouth to make sure he hadn't left it in by mistake. But the tooth was nowhere to be found. He'd have to preach the Sunday sermon without it.

Unfortunately, when the preacher spoke without his tooth, a whistling sound came out of his mouth at every word containing the letter s. Come sermon time, he found himself preaching about the "bottomlesss pitsss of hell." Out came the whistle. The congregation, which was supposed to be very serious, couldn't keep from giggling. "What'sss ssso funny?" asked the preacher. "All I sssaid wasss the bottom-lesss pitsss of hell." The congregation giggled again.

After the service, quite red-faced, the preacher got ready to move on to the next parish. He pleaded with the farmer and his wife, "Pleassse find that tooth of mine. I need it, and it wasss very exssspensssive. I can't afford to replassse it."

"All I can imagine," said the farmer, "is that one of the chickens got to it, thinking it was a kernel of corn."

"Well, how many chickens do you have?" asked the preacher.

"Twenty," said the farmer.

"I don't exssspect you to find my tooth immediately," said the preacher. "But I hope you'll examine the gizzsssard of every chicken you eat."

A month passed. Then, one day the preacher received a letter with the tooth inside:

Dear Reverend Hays,

Good news! We finally found your tooth. Would you believe it was in the twentieth chicken? The very last one. Our family never ate so well!

This story is from the family history of my friend Lee Hays. Lee was from Arkansas and he had so many good stories that I find myself still telling them. Some of the funniest, like this one, were about his father.

I guess there were all kinds of folks like my parents and Lee's, wandering America's countryside in the first few decades of the twentieth century, preaching and singing for their supper. And like my father's story "The Trailer and the Flood," Lee's story is plain old family history.

It's not only entertaining, it's important for kids to hear that their parents and grandparents have made mistakes, bloopers, and blunders as we all do, and survived to tell the tale. Yesss, even our familiesss' mythic figuresss are sssusssceptible to human comedy.

TAKASHI OHTA
CROSSES THE OCEAN

IN 1911, at the age of nineteen, Takashi Ohta left Japan.

Takashi's father spoke for people when the government didn't treat them fairly, and the leaders of Japan did not like what he was doing. They sentenced Takashi's father to exile. That is, they told him to leave the country. But he had a small business to keep afloat and a large family to support.

The only alternative was the ancient Japanese tradition that a son could take his father's banishment. Takashi was young and strong and an expert at judo. He told his father, "I can go in your place. You stay with the family."

He bowed low to his parents and bade good-bye to his brothers and sisters and his nieces and nephews. And he set off.

Takashi's first stop was China. He joined a military unit and fought under the Chinese leader Sun Yat-sen. When his unit was defeated, all of the soldiers fled to the hills.

There Takashi met up with a group of traveling Japanese Buddhist monks who were looking for a bodyguard. The monks were on their way to Lhasa, the capital of Tibet, to seek the help of the head lama in settling an obscure theological argument. Takashi told them, "I am a black belt in judo. I can protect you."

So Takashi shaved his head, put on a robe, and became their bodyguard. He walked with the monks two thousand miles, over the Gobi Desert and up through mountain passes and high valleys. Can you imagine such a journey? It took a whole year. But as he promised, Takashi protected the monks on the entire journey to Tibet.

From Tibet, Takashi made his way down to the coast of India, where he found a job peeling potatoes on a British merchant ship. And for the next several years that's how he earned his keep. He sailed to South Africa. He sailed to the Mediterranean.

On one voyage in the Mediterranean, his ship worked alongside a Japanese naval boat. This was during World War I when Japan was on the same side as England. The

British admiral wanted to have a conference with the Japanese admiral but discovered that he needed an interpreter. "Sir," said an officer, "I believe there's a Japanese man who works below in the galley peeling potatoes. Maybe he can translate."

"Get him up here on the double," said the British admiral. "But make sure he's presentable."

So the British dressed Takashi up in a suit of clothes and brought him up on deck. Takashi did a fine job as interpreter, but his moment above deck didn't last long. When the meeting was done, the suit of clothes was taken away, and Takashi was sent back down to peel potatoes.

When the ship arrived in Brazil, Takashi got off. He wanted to try something new and found a job with a company cutting a way for the railroad through a jungle. As might be expected, the local Indians were not pleased with the railroad coming through their land. The railroad company decided that Takashi should represent them because they thought he looked a little bit like the Indians. Once again, Takashi found himself serving as the intermediary between two cultures.

The Indians seemed to take a real liking to Takashi until he made an innocent mistake. He gave an Indian girl a gift, a little doll made from straw. He didn't know that the girl was engaged to be married. Her fiancé became furiously jealous.

The next day, the young man hid a rattlesnake in Takashi's lunch box. When Takashi reached in for his lunch, the snake bit him. His fellow workers fed him whiskey and rum for three days, the only treatment available. Takashi recovered, but from that day on he complained about not being able to smell quite so well. Whether this was due to the snakebite or all the whiskey, he never knew.

Eventually, Takashi rejoined a ship. He spent a total of three years sailing on British merchant ships before arriving in the United States. The year was 1919, and by that time, Takashi never wanted to see another potato again.

But the story doesn't end here. In 1963, fifty-two years after he had left Japan, Takashi returned to see his brothers and sisters. Because he was the oldest surviving male, his sister knelt down in front of him with her face touching the floor. "Sister," he said, "please rise." He knew that she would not rise until he said so. This was the Japanese custom.

Soon she felt relaxed enough to ask something she was curious about. "Tell me, Brother, is it true that people in America sit in the same bathwater they wash their bodies in?"

"Yes, Sister, they do," answered Takashi.

"How disgusting!" exclaimed the sister. "You don't do anything like that, do you, Brother?"

"Oh, I would never, Sister," Takashi replied. He knew that the Japanese would never use soap in the same bathwater they used for soaking. First they wash and rinse, and only then do they sit in a big hot tub, sometimes with friends, where they can talk and relax.

Takashi could not admit that after forty-four years of American life he did not bathe like a Japanese person. He knew then just how American he had become.

⟵——

This is the "across-the-ocean" story of my wife's father. It's just a short sketch. Takashi actually wrote an entire book about his travels, called The Golden Wind.

These tales are plentiful in America. Whether our relations arrived by water, air, or land, we are mostly a country of immigrants. Such life-altering journeys make for great stories.

Family and personal history are especially popular these days. Memoirs and biographies flow out of bookstores, family reunions mark people's calendars, and family trees blossom on the

Internet. But as interesting as novels, picnics, and computers can be, they're not the only way to explore and celebrate family heritage. All you really need is a listener and your own memory. "Did I ever tell you about Great-Grandpa and Great-Grandma and how they came to America? It's really quite exciting. . . ."

SOME AMERICAN STRUGGLES

The Down Rent Wars

IN THE EARLY 1840S, a small revolution took place in up-state New York. It was known as the "Down Rent Wars." Ever hear of it?

Ever since the days when New York was called New Amsterdam, thousands of farmers had worked the land of the Hudson River Valley. But they did so without ever having the opportunity to own the land. Most of the valley belonged to a few big "patroons." *Patroon* is a Dutch term for the owner of an estate. One patroon, Stephen Van Rensselaer III, owned two million acres of land. Sixty thousand tenant farmers had to treat him like a feudal lord and pay an annual rent to farm his land. The tenants even had to bow whenever Van Rensselaer's carriage passed.

The 1840s were an exciting decade. The abolitionist movement, the temperance movement, the women's suffrage movement, and the union movement all got their start around this time. And during this same period, the farmers near Albany started an organization to strike against unfair land rents.

They called themselves the "Calico Indians," and like the participants in the Boston Tea Party, they painted their faces to conceal their identities. But such organizations were illegal, so the Calico Indians had to keep their membership secret. They wore calico robes, met at night, and to signal each other, used the long tin horns that were used to call workers in from the fields.

When a sheriff arrived to evict a farmer for not paying his rent, he would find the Calico Indians lying in wait, guns in hand. They'd surround him, then burn the eviction papers.

In some of these confrontations, people got hurt. In Greene County, near Albany, one sheriff, Big Bill Snyder, was killed. A song was written about it, set to the popular tune of "Old Dan Tucker":

Keep out the way, Big Bill Snyder,

We'll tar your coat and feather your hide, sir.

Now at the beginning of the Down Rent Wars, the newspapers and leading political parties had nothing but condemnation for the violent tactics used by the farmers. Hundreds of farmers were jailed, and their main leader was sentenced to be hung. But because the farmers put up a struggle, they gained some publicity about their economic situation. News about their cause spread around the state.

It wasn't long before the citizens of New York State began to say, "It doesn't seem fair that these people have been farming the land for two hundred years and still have to pay high rents to the patroon. This isn't what America is supposed to be about. One person shouldn't own two million acres of land." And as public opinion changed, the politicians changed. They also began to say, "What's happening to these farmers doesn't seem fair."

Come the next election, both political parties vowed to change the New York State constitution to force the breakup of the big estates. And that's exactly what happened. New York's next governor won on just such a promise.

So even though the farmers started their struggle with violence, they eventually won it peacefully at the ballot box.

The Coal Creek Rebellion

DOWN IN EASTERN TENNESSEE during the late 1880s, coal miners, like the New York farmers before them, struggled against unbearable working conditions. But when the miners began talking about a union, the coal company made a deal with the governor of Tennessee to get state prisoners to do the miner's job. There's a song about this struggle, too. It's known as "Roll Down the Line":

Way back yonder in Tennessee, they leased the convicts out.

Put them working in the mine, against free labor stout.

In 1892 the miners stood their ground and refused to sign an unfair contract. A group of them in the town of Coal Creek put their heads together. "What are we going to do about this prison labor? It's not fair that convict labor should take the place of free labor. We're just asking for decent working conditions." The miners signed a petition saying there was no way they could compete with prison labor. But the governor and the Tennessee Coal and Iron Company didn't pay any attention.

One dark night, a group of miners armed themselves. Many of them were veterans of the Civil War. Some had been Union Army men and some had been Confederate Army men. They went down to the prison stockade, surrounded it, and told the warden, "Release those prisoners or we'll burn the stockade down with you inside." The warden surrendered, and the prisoners were set free and quickly ran off.

But the governor in Nashville wasn't about to give in to a bunch of coal miners. Again, he sent prisoners to work the mines. And this time the state militia came as an escort. The presence of the troops made the miners even angrier. They marched down to the stockade, surrounded it, and freed the prisoners once again.

Three times the rebels freed the prisoners; three times the troops recaptured the convicts or brought in others. The Coal Creek Rebellion dragged on for nearly three years. Some of the leaders were jailed. Others were forced into hiding. It got so bad that the state couldn't collect taxes from some of those eastern mining counties.

Finally, the miners took irreversible action. They burned

down the stockade. And to prevent the prisoners from being recaptured, they hid them in their homes and gave them civilian clothing. They even helped the convicts escape across the state border.

With all this ruckus, the miners' cause began attracting attention. Newspapers in Memphis, Nashville, Chattanooga, and Knoxville began to say, "It doesn't seem right that prison labor is competing with free labor." Then the public took the miners' cause to heart.

At the next election, a new governor was voted into office on the promise to ban the use of convict labor. And in 1894, that's what Tennessee did.

Rosa Parks and Martin Luther King, Jr.

THIS STORY IS only a small part of a very big story. One of the biggest stories of struggle in our country's history.

Nearly a hundred years had passed since the end of the Civil War. But from Texas to Maryland, Florida to Arkansas, African Americans still lived as second-class citizens, in spite of heroes like Frederick Douglass, Harriet Tubman, and W. E. B. Du Bois.

Voting? Forget it.

Schools? Segregated.

Jim Crow laws ruled the South.

These laws meant blacks and whites had separate drinking fountains, separate toilets, separate restaurants, and black people could only ride in the back of public buses. But in 1955 something happened.

In the state of Tennessee, an education center called the Highlander Folk School sponsored a small conference. The topic was how black people and white people could work together to change race relations in the South.

A woman, a seamstress by trade, had come to the conference from Alabama to see what she might learn. She was interested in the topic, but skeptical of what the conference had to offer.

At the end of the weeklong session, the director, Myles Horton, asked each participant: "What are you going to do when you get home to put into practice what you've learned here?"

One person said, "I'm going to start a voter registration drive. I think I know the steps I've got to take, and I'm going to take them."

Another person answered, "I think I've got to start before that. I'm going to begin literacy classes. Some of my neighbors don't know how to read and write. I've picked up some ideas this week and I'm going to put them to use."

Finally, it was the seamstress's turn. "Well," she said, "I don't know what I'm going to do."

The others pressed her, "You must have some idea."

"I don't know just yet," she answered. "But I'm going to do something."

A month later, in her hometown of Montgomery, Alabama, she did do something. Riding home one afternoon on a crowded city bus, she refused to give up her seat to a white passenger. Her name was Rosa Parks.

Well, Rosa Parks was arrested, put in jail, and allowed one phone call. She called her friend, E. D. Nixon. Nixon was astounded. "Rosa, what are you doing in jail?"

"I refused to give up my seat," said Parks. "The police arrested me."

"That's outrageous. I'll be down right away to bail you out." And that's what he did.

Now, this might not have come to much if it hadn't been for a coincidence. An extraordinary young preacher had just come to Montgomery to head up a prosperous church. Nixon had heard this new preacher speak and was impressed. He had never heard anybody speak with such authority and poetry. Nixon started to make some phone calls.

First, he called the NAACP in Washington, D.C. "Everybody knows Rosa Parks. She wouldn't hurt a fly. She's a very well respected person. I bet her story could unite the community."

"That's very interesting, Mr. Nixon," they said. "We'll discuss it at our meeting next week."

"Next week?" said Nixon. "We've got to move *now.*" He called his union leader, A. Philip Randolph. Nixon was a sleeping-car porter and Randolph had been head of the porters' union.

"You're right," said Randolph. "This could unite the community. Don't waste a minute. Have you got a pencil and paper? Here are a few suggestions."

Nixon took notes, and one of the people he called next was the new preacher.

"You want to use our church as a meeting place?" asked the preacher. "Well, Brother Nixon, as you know I'm new here. I'd better check with my deacons. Call me back in two hours."

When Nixon called back two hours later, the preacher said, "I'm very glad to tell you that the deacons have approved your request. We can use the church for a meeting tonight."

"I'm so glad you've said that, Reverend King," Nixon

replied. "Because I've already told two hundred people that we're meeting at your church at eight o'clock."

As you might have guessed, the preacher's name was Martin Luther King, Jr. And as they do with any large meeting, the city newspaper covered the story. It appeared in the Sunday paper. People formed the Montgomery Improvement Association and agreed to organize a boycott of the city transit system until it was desegregated.

Monday morning arrived. The preacher's wife, Coretta, said, "Wake up, Martin! Three buses have gone by and not a single person is on them."

There's a song about this, too:

If you miss me at the back of the bus

And you can't find me nowhere,

Oh, come on over to the front of the bus,

I'll be riding up there.

The rest is history.

Have you ever thought about how many confrontations have started with threats and fists and ended with handshakes and *compromise? At numerous times in American history, groups of people have felt themselves so wronged that they decide to take drastic action to create change. And often these groups have succeeded only when they find ways to get their message heard. The price of liberty is eternal publicity.*

However—and it's a big however—public awareness did not help Native Americans in their struggles to keep their homelands. Public awareness did not help Africans in any one of their three hundred slave revolts in America. But in the mid twentieth century the struggles of African Americans did change dramatically with the arrival of the Reverend Martin Luther King, Jr., who, using the principles of nonviolence, won respect from all people. His peaceful protests spread his message and made news around the world.

Here's a personal example of an American struggle right here in my own Hudson River neighborhood. In the early sixties I fell in love with sailing. I had a job out on Cape Cod and somebody took me out in a sailboat. When I returned home to New York, I wanted to sail on the Hudson, but I discovered that much of the river was like an open sewer. What could be done?

A friend of mine, Vic Schwartz, told me about the large sailboats called "sloops" that once hauled bricks and other cargo on the river. Vic and I got an unusual bunch of folks together, raised some money, and three years later the sloop Clearwater was launched.

This beautiful sailboat was so striking, it immediately caught the eye and sparked interest. It started getting its picture in the papers and on TV. I was even on the Tonight Show and Johnny Carson asked, "What's going to be the name of this boat?" When I said, "Clearwater," he said, "On the Hudson? Ha, ha, ha." Everybody laughed, and rightly so, at the time. But we worked hard, got publicity for the Clearwater, raised money, and most importantly, raised awareness about issues affecting the Hudson through educational sails, river festivals, and working with other like-minded organizations.

Today people are enjoying the river again. Swimming is safe from Catskill to Yonkers. And every year the Clearwater takes twenty-thousand schoolchildren and adults out, fifty at a time, showing them that a clean and healthy river is a resource for us all.

I'm sure you have your own examples. Maybe you're active on your local school board or in local politics. Maybe you've fought for a new playground and won or succeeded in getting cars to slow down at a busy intersection. Whatever the specific struggle, people working together toward a positive change make for a good story.

5 *A Few of My Own Stories*

WHEN IT COMES to improvising your own stories, imagine that anything is possible. This is what my father did when he made up stories like "The Foolish Frog." A frog that can talk? The impossibility adds to the story's appeal.

One way to get started is simply to ask, "What would happen if...?" What would happen if lightbulbs could talk? What would happen if a magic potion could make things as thin as paper? These are two of the questions that sparked the stories in this section. Of course, each of us will come up with different answers to these questions, but that's to be expected. Imaginations are like fingerprints. They are unique.

Like any part of the body, imaginations need exercise. But more often than not, we don't give them a good work-out. We have TV dinners so we don't have to think about cooking; packaged vacations so we don't have to think about traveling; prefab homes so we don't have to think about building. It seems most of the adventure has been taken out of everyday life. This is one reason I like to make up stories about the unexpected, the unbelievable, and the previously unimagined. And if my listeners say, "Hmmm, I never thought of that," I know their imaginations have gotten a little exercise.

The possibilities are endless if you let your imagination go. But be patient. Not every story you make up will be a smash hit. Improvised stories may have an unwieldy quirkiness. They'll have edges and bumps and meanderings like any homemade thing. Your audience's reaction will tell you when you've hit upon something wonderful. It's either, "Not that story again!" or "Tell it one more time!"

If you live in a big city, you can make up a story about city life. Every city has highways, railroads, and airports. Imagine an adventure using one of these avenues and add in a character or two. What if two long-lost friends met at the station? Where are they going? Where are they coming from? What if the two friends weren't people at all, but pigeons? If you live in the suburbs, you can make up a story about your particular neighborhood. What if a squirrel stole birdseed from the feeder? What if the squirrel got rich selling the seed back to the birds? Or maybe you live in the country, and there's a bush that blooms pale blue blossoms every spring. What if one year it bloomed bright orange?

When I was a kid, most stories had one basic message: If you're strong, if you're brave, if you're honest, everything will turn out all right. It's a good message, but we can add other important messages. One I include quite often is that if we work together, we can accomplish things that we can't do alone. Another is that if the world is going to last, we must make better choices about how we live. And if we all do our part, a hundred years from now our grandchildren will be making up their own stories and retelling the ones we're making up today.

THE LITTLE BASEBALL MAN

A FAMILY LIVED on the side of a small mountain. One day the father was driving home from work when he came upon a little man with a long white beard. Next to the man stood a sign: BASEBALLS: FIVE CENTS.

"Wow," said the father. "Just what I need!" He and his son were always losing baseballs in the bushes near their house. "I'll stop and buy a few," he thought.

"Greetings to you, sir," said the little man.

"Hello," said the father. "Some fine baseballs you've got here."

"The finest," said the little man. He was sitting on a log whittling a beautiful walking stick.

"My son, Tommy, just started Little League," said the father, "so I'm always on the lookout for a good baseball."

"Look no further," said the little man.

"Then I'll take three," said the father.

As he examined the baseballs more closely, he realized they were slightly used, but still in excellent condition.

"That'll be fifteen cents," said the little man.

"Are you sure? Only five cents apiece?" asked the father. "How can you sell them at such a price?"

"Well, I like to go hiking all around here," said the little man. "And on my walks I pick up all sorts of things. You wouldn't believe what people drop: mittens and keys and every kind of trash! Bottles, cans, gum wrappers, plastic containers. You name it, I've picked it up. But this year, seems I've been finding baseballs. Every time I look under the bushes on the far side of this mountain, I'm sure to find one or two. I like to pass the savings on to my customers."

So there the father was, buying back his own baseballs! But he didn't want to hurt the little man's feelings. So he paid him anyway. He imagined the little man must live on things like wild mushrooms, sassafras tea, and maple syrup and, like anybody else, long for a little variety once in a while. Maybe a special occasion was coming up, like his birthday, and he was saving up his nickels to buy himself a soda pop.

"Well, thanks," said the father.

"No, thank *you*," said the little man. "Only fifty more cents and I can happily retire."

"*Retire?*" asked the father in surprise.

"Yes, I'm buying a sailboat and sailing around the world."

Life is filled with unsolved mysteries like disappearing socks and mittens or toys that vanish into thin air. I used to tell this particular story to my son, Danny, back when he was involved in Little League. From time to time, we'd lose a baseball in the bushes up here on the mountain and we'd have to drive into town to buy another one. The two of us got to wondering where all those baseballs disappeared to.

"The Little Baseball Man" is a very basic story. I use the familiar folktale character of a little magic man to help explain a situation particular to me and my son. Of course, if your children don't play baseball, you can substitute socks, mittens, keys, hair ties, or anything else. And if you live in a city, why not change the mountain to a city block? As with any story, don't hesitate to fiddle with the recipe to make it fit your tastes.

THE INTELLIGENT
LIGHTBULBS

THERE WAS ONCE a brilliant scientist who worked night and day trying to unravel the great questions of the universe. But before he could finish, his brain got overloaded, and he collapsed from exhaustion.

His doctor told him, "You need to take a break from science. Work with your hands instead of your brain. The mind is nothing without a healthy body."

The scientist followed his doctor's advice and took a job in a lightbulb factory. His job was to take the lightbulbs off the conveyor belt, wrap them in padding, and put them into cardboard boxes. As the weeks passed, his doctor encouraged him: "You're getting better. Keep up the good work."

Now, in big factories that produce thousands of things like lightbulbs, each thing is supposed to be exactly the same. But sometimes accidents occur.

It so happened that the scientist liked to talk to the light-bulbs as one might talk to houseplants. There was only one problem. The bulbs went by too quickly on the conveyor belt. The conversations were brief and very impersonal. "Hello," he'd say. "Good-bye," he'd say. So it wasn't long before he lifted a box of bulbs off the belt and kept them at his side for company. Throughout his shift he'd tell them poems and jokes and stories.

One day, a large order for lightbulbs came in to the factory. Every last box of bulbs was needed to fill the order, including the ones the scientist had kept out. "I'll be sad to see you go, my little friends, but I have no choice," he told them. He patted the top of each bulb and sent them on their way. The next morning, the bulbs were delivered to a distant high school and installed in classroom 2B, the one used for English classes.

At first, there was no noticeable difference between these bulbs and the other lightbulbs in the school. But one evening, after a few months, the night janitor heard voices that seemed to be coming from classroom 2B. "Did somebody leave a radio on?" the janitor wondered. He looked everywhere in the classroom: beneath desks, in closets, behind filing cabinets. Finally, he threw down his broom in frustration and asked, "Where's that conversation coming from?"

"Up here," replied the voices.

"Come out this instant," demanded the janitor. "School has been over for hours."

"We can't come out. You have to unscrew us," said the voices.

The janitor looked up. He got a stepladder and put his ear to the ceiling. "Am I out of my nut, or are you lightbulbs talking?"

"We're discussing, not talking. We've been here all year and we were just going over tonight's homework when you interrupted us."

"Pardon me," said the janitor, "but I've never met talking lightbulbs before."

"Please don't tell anyone," the lightbulbs asked.

"Who could I tell?" said the janitor. "No one would believe me."

"Just the same," said the lightbulbs. "Please keep this to yourself. And if it's no bother, could you move us to another classroom? Preferably mathematics."

"Mathematics?" asked the janitor.

"Yes, we hear students complain about algebra and plane geometry, but we think math sounds very interesting."

"I must be losing my mind," said the janitor, "but what

harm could it do?" So that evening, he carefully unscrewed all four lightbulbs and exchanged them with the bulbs in the math room.

Over the next few months, the lightbulbs studied extra hard. The more they learned, the more intelligent they became. "We wonder if we could get some more variety in our classes?" they asked the janitor one day. "Sooner or later, we'll want to graduate. How about taking us to the physics class?"

So that evening, the janitor carefully unscrewed all four lightbulbs and exchanged them with the bulbs in the physics room. As their knowledge of physics grew, the lightbulbs started to become impatient when students didn't pay attention or do their homework.

One day, the physics teacher asked a simple question about electrical currents. None of the students knew the answer. The lightbulbs tried to stay quiet, but they couldn't. Finally, they blurted out the answer.

"Well, at least *somebody* is paying attention," said the physics teacher. "Who is it? Raise your hand."

But nobody moved.

"I heard somebody give the answer," said the teacher.

Again, complete silence. After a minute, a young man

raised his hand and said meekly, "I think the answer came from up there." He pointed to the ceiling. The other students giggled.

"Oh, really?" questioned the teacher. "I suppose the answer came from a little bird or a talking ceiling tile? Or perhaps an intelligent lightbulb?" Everybody laughed. "Not likely," they thought.

But after dismissing the class, the physics teacher distinctly heard voices discussing that evening's homework. She checked the hallway. It was empty except for the janitor. "Strange," she said. "I thought I heard voices."

The janitor just leaned on his broom and scratched his head. "I've been hearing voices in this school for years," he said.

"But these voices were discussing tonight's physics assignment very intelligently," said the teacher.

Suddenly, a voice blurted out, "Well, it's no wonder we're good at physics. We've been in this class for weeks. Won't you please move us to another class so we can learn enough to graduate?"

"*Shhh!*" hushed the janitor, hurrying into the classroom. "Do you want to be discovered?"

"Who are you talking to?" asked the teacher.

"I can't say," moaned the janitor.

"I promise not to tell," said the teacher.

And the voice from the ceiling asked, "Is that a real promise?"

"Why, yes, it's a real promise," said the astonished teacher.

"Then we're pleased to meet you," said the lightbulbs.

And over the following months, the physics teacher helped the janitor move the lightbulbs from one classroom to another. The bulbs learned Spanish and chemistry and all the things that high school students must learn in order to graduate.

By late spring the lightbulbs had received an excellent high school education and were no longer afraid to let everybody know about it. At graduation, the principal gave diplomas to all four of the extraordinary lightbulbs, and the Employee of the Year Award to the janitor.

And believe it or not, the lightbulbs received scholarships to college. One became a world-famous professor. The others became research experts and, with their unique perspective, solved many problems that human beings had found impossible, including one of the very problems that had plagued the scientist at the beginning of our story.

By working in the lightbulb factory the scientist had made a major contribution to the world of science after all!

The world is a much healthier place when everyone has a contribution to make, and the scientist in this story serves as a good example. He doesn't single-handedly solve the world's problems, but he does his job thoughtfully and with care, as do the janitor and the physics teacher. They all play a role in bringing about solutions.

We live in a culture that emphasizes the superstar and the hero, and it's easy to forget how vital it is that each one of us does our own part, however small and insignificant it may seem. Think what we can do for the world if we all recycle our own morning newspapers, pick up our own candy wrappers, and conserve what water we can.

Now, what about the plausibility of these talking lightbulbs? Impossible, you say. But the world would never amount to a hill of beans if people didn't use their imaginations to think of the impossible. An enormous metal bird with hundreds of passengers flying through the sky? Impossible. Speaking into a gadget to a friend halfway around the globe? Impossible. Why not talking lightbulbs?

I often use "The Intelligent Lightbulbs" in schools when I urge kids to make up their own stories using whatever they find around them. I point to the lights overhead and ask, "Did you ever stop to think what would happen if lightbulbs could actually listen and learn? After all, they've been in this classroom a long time. . . ."

THE DEAF MUSICIANS

MANY YEARS AGO, there lived a jazz musician who was losing his hearing. His friends tried to cheer him up, but it was obvious to everybody that his days as a professional piano player were over.

This musician lived in New York City, and when his hearing had all but disappeared, his doctor referred him to a special school in Brooklyn that taught sign language and lipreading.

A few months into his studies, the piano player met another student who had been a jazz clarinetist. The two instantly became good friends, and together they rode the subway back and forth to school. And because they spoke in sign language, conversation was easy despite the racket of the subway cars and the noise of the rush-hour crowds.

One evening, riding home on the subway, they got to rec-ollecting a famous jazz recording. Using their hands to re-play the song, they discovered they could follow each other perfectly. Each musician heard the music in his own mind: the piano player heard his piano; the clarinet player heard his clarinet. It wasn't long before they were recollecting other tunes, and their little jam sessions got to be a regular occur-rence there on the subway as it bounced and rattled along.

On one particular trip, a woman approached them with a broad smile. "I know this song!" her smile said, and she began to play the stand-up bass. Only she had no bass. Her left hand moved up and down through the air while her right hand made the plucking motions. All three musi-cians—the piano player, the clarinet player, and the bass player—laughed and played excitedly.

Soon the jazz trio had regular rehearsals on the subway, and with each rehearsal they got better and better. Com-muters started to give them an audience. Some people even missed their stops just to stay and watch.

"All we need now is a vocalist," the clarinet player signed one evening.

"I've got just the person," signed the bass player. She had a friend who was a sign-language interpreter and knew all the jazz standards by heart. She was added to the group, and when the musicians played, the interpreter signed the songs with such great emotion, tears would come to passengers' eyes.

Now, some people would believe that with so many complications and obstacles, the silent jazz quartet would eventually have to break up.

But it didn't happen that way.

Their subway concerts became famous throughout New York City. And just when they thought their careers were over, the deaf musicians ended up playing to the most enthusiastic audiences of their careers.

Although I've never played with deaf musicians, each year I participate in a music festival called the Great Hudson River Revival. One of its long-standing traditions is to have a sign-language interpreter on every music stage. It's a reminder of the power of music even when it can't be heard.

This story touches on a couple of interesting ideas: First, that an important aspect of art is what goes on in the mind of the artist, not in the final production. We're taught pretty early that only a few people can call themselves painters, singers, musicians, dancers, or storytellers, when, really, these are basic human activities, open to all of us. The musicians in this story are musicians even if they don't produce one audible tone.

The second idea is that the power of people working together is itself a kind of magic. Musical ensembles are a great example of this: Each individual does his or her part to create a beautiful whole. I've seen this at concerts when I get an audience singing a song—the altos take one part, the tenors take another, and other folks fill in between until there's a thunderous, joyful sound, something much greater than the song I began.

THE MAGIC THINNER

ONE SUMMER MORNING, Miss Sally and her grand-daughter, Mary, were passing by the antique store on their way to the train. An old-fashioned laundry wringer sat in the front display window.

"Morning, Miss Sally," said Joseph, the shop owner, as he swept the sidewalk.

"Morning, Joseph. That's a fine old wringer you've got there."

"Yes, ma'am, I just put it in the window," said Joseph.

"Mary, see that gizmo with the two rubber rollers and a hand crank?" said Miss Sally. "That's a wringer. They used to stand in many a kitchen."

Mary pulled on Miss Sally's hand. "Grandma, we're going to miss the train."

But Miss Sally didn't budge. Her eyes were fixed on the

wringer. "We used them to squeeze the water out of the clothes before hanging the wash on the line," she said.

"Let's go, Grandma," said Mary.

"Now hold on," said Miss Sally. "Did I ever tell you how I saved the world?"

"Grandma, there's no time for stories."

Miss Sally turned to Joseph. "This young one wants to rush me everywhere," she said.

"I see that," said Joseph. "Don't worry about that train, though. Those new engines are always late."

But wouldn't you know it? When they got to the station, they found their train was not only late, it had been canceled. "These new engines are always having mechanical troubles," sighed the stationmaster. "Next train will be in an hour."

Miss Sally and Mary sat down on a bench to wait. "OK, Grandma, now tell me how you saved the world," said Mary.

"I thought there wasn't any time for stories," said Miss Sally.

"Oh, Grandma, go on. Tell it."

And so Miss Sally leaned back, closed her eyes, and the words came to her, as they always did, with great ease. . . .

In the time before television, just after the Second World War, I was just about your age. My father had a job as a chemist with a large company. He was the first person in the family to graduate from college and get such a job, but we still could only afford a tiny three-room apartment. There was a front room, a kitchen, and a bedroom.

It was on the fourth floor of a walk-up, and I remember each and every one of those steps. *Clip, clop. Clip, clop.* One step had a corner broken off. Another step had a long scratch. My, how the sounds carried in that stairwell! My feet sounded like an old horse going up those stairs. *Clip, clop. Clip, clop.*

One day I came home from school, and there wasn't a soul to greet me, except for my little dog, Bongo. He was so excited, he jumped up on my legs, his tail wagging this way and that way. "Bongo, no jumping," I scolded. "And don't get underfoot."

A note from my parents was on the table:

We'll be back by suppertime. Don't go out.

It didn't matter whether I wanted to go out or not. It was raining, and I mean hard. I tried riding my tricycle around the kitchen, but the room was too crowded. What with the table and chairs and the big washtub with the laundry wringer on it (just like the one in Joseph's display window), I kept bumping into everything. I tried playing with my toys, but nothing seemed agreeable.

Then I tried playing my father's accordion. He'd been teaching me a lovely new tune. I gave the accordion a few squeezes and pulls.

Outside, I could hear our neighbor, Sailor John, playing one of his pretty rain tunes on his concertina, a kind of small accordion. As a young man, he'd been a sailor, scrambling up masts of great ships. The rain seemed to make him think of the sea. I called down to him and waved, and he nodded back.

But after a few minutes, the accordion got too heavy for me, and I put it down.

I pulled out my chemistry set. I wasn't supposed to fool with it without my parents around, but I was so bored I had to do something. I'd been working on something I called "disappearing ink." But the only thing it had done was stain the tablecloth.

Out of curiosity, I took the entire bottle of my disappearing ink and poured it into the washtub. Then I found a bottle of vanishing cream on my mother's dresser and I added that to the tub. Next, I found a big can of paint thinner and I added that to the tub. In my father's photography equipment, I found something called "reducing agent," and I poured in the whole bottle. I also threw in a few diet pills from the medicine cabinet. Finally, I topped the mixture off with several gallons of distilled water, stirred it around and around, and stepped back.

Smoke and steam rose up from the tub! Bongo let out a whimper and scrambled beneath the table. I picked up the first thing I saw, my father's old catcher's mitt, and dipped it in. But nothing happened. It didn't disappear. It just came out as soggy as a sponge.

I was worried that the mitt wouldn't dry before my parents got home, so I got the idea to run it through the wringer. Would you believe it? The mitt came out the other side as thin as a piece of paper. It looked like a cutout of a mitt.

Next, I tried one of my mother's dresses. I put it in the tub, then ran it through the wringer. Out it came looking like a dress for a big paper doll. I tried more and more things. What had been my father's overcoat became a long, damp silhouette of an overcoat.

I ran into the bedroom and grabbed a pillow. I put that in the tub. It came out sopping wet. I ran it through the wringer and out it came, flat as paper. I thinned lamps and end tables. I thinned almost everything in the kitchen.

Now I had plenty of space to ride my tricycle. But as I walked around the near-empty room, I wondered, "How can I get everything back to its original shape?" I hadn't thought of that.

I tried blowing the thinned items up like balloons, but I only got out of breath. I tried shaking them out, but I only got sore arms. Then I spotted my father's accordion. I thought of the tune he had been teaching me. It had a real expansive feel to it, like you'd want to stand up and fill your lungs. That gave me an idea.

I picked up the thin, paperlike pillow and tucked it into the folds of the accordion. Then I pushed the accordion in, and pulled it out—*Dee-dee, da-da*—trying to play the lovely tune. Then *plop,* down on the floor fell a big, fat pillow. "Unbelievable!" I thought.

I tried other items: a typewriter, a book, a metal pail. After I tucked them into the folds of the accordion and drew out one long chord, they all returned to their regular shape.

Now I went through the rest of the apartment. I dipped

one item after another into the magic thinner: my father's bowling ball, my mother's sewing basket. Anything I could find, I ran through the wringer. Pretty soon the apartment was completely bare except for Bongo and the pile of thinned items in the corner. Now I could ride my tricycle through the parlor, then back through the kitchen, and into the bedroom. I was having so much fun, I didn't hear my parents' footsteps.

The next thing I knew, the door was open and my mother was gasping, "Where on earth is everything?"

"Mama! Papa! I've made the greatest invention," I shouted.

"Forget your inventions, young lady," scolded my mother. "Where are our things?"

"Mama, you know how crowded this apartment is," I said. "It doesn't have to be!" I grabbed my father's briefcase and put it into the magic thinner.

"Hey, that's important!" cried my father.

"Don't worry," I said, as I ran his briefcase through the wringer. "See? Thin as paper!"

"Sally, what kind of nonsense is this?" asked my father. "Where is my briefcase?"

"Just watch," I said. Then I folded the briefcase into the creases of the accordion and played the tune—*Dee-dee, da-da.* Out plopped the briefcase in its original shape.

My father quickly snatched it up and leafed through it. "Everything's here. I can't believe it. Sally, this is extraordinary!"

"Now when it rains," I said, "Bongo and I will have a place to play."

"This is much bigger than you think," said my father. "If businesses could store their products as thin as paper, they wouldn't have to rent as much space. Fortunes will be saved. I'll call my company's lawyer right away."

Soon the company lawyer arrived. My father grabbed the lawyer's hat off his head.

"Hey, that's my best hat!" cried the lawyer. I ran it through the magic thinner and wringer and handed him the newly thinned hat.

"Hmmm, I wouldn't believe it if I hadn't seen it with my own eyes," said the lawyer, turning the paper-thin hat over in his hands.

"Sally," my father said proudly, "show him what else your invention can do."

I folded the thinned hat into the accordion and started playing—*Dee-dee, da-da.* Out fell the lawyer's fine hat, good as new.

"Incredible!" said the lawyer, more cheerfully. "Have you told anyone else about this?"

"No," said my father. "Only you."

"Perfect," said the lawyer. "I know just who to call. By chance, he's in town." The lawyer dialed the telephone. "Hello, General? Listen, you must see me immediately. It could be vital to national security."

Soon the general arrived, and I demonstrated my invention again, using the general's hat this time.

"Astonishing," said the general. "My dear little girl, you have invented something that will tip the scales of power. We'll be able to ship entire army divisions in one plane. It does work on humans, doesn't it?"

I shrugged my shoulders. "I don't know."

"Get in that tub," the general barked at the lawyer. "On the double!"

"Now, wait a minute," said the lawyer. "Don't you think we should test it on an animal first?" And before anybody could say a word, the lawyer scooped Bongo up and threw him in.

"How dare you!" screamed my mother. But that didn't stop the lawyer. He snatched Bongo out of the tub and ran him through the wringer.

The general handed me a paper-thin Bongo. "Here, my dear, bring him back."

With tears streaming down my cheeks, I folded Bongo into the accordion and played—*Dee-dee, da-da.* But nothing happened. *Dee-dee, da-da.* I tried over and over again, but for all my efforts, nothing worked. Then I was crying so hard I couldn't play anymore.

"There, there, little girl," said the general. "We'll get you ten more little dogs. Too bad your invention doesn't work on living things, but it's valuable just the same. Now, what did you put in that tub?"

"I don't know and I don't care!" I yelled. "I want Bongo!" I ran to the washtub and tipped it over. The magic thinner sank right into the floor. Smoke and steam rose up.

"Now there's nothing left to analyze!" shouted the general. "I could have been the most powerful general in the world!"

"And I could have been president!" shouted the lawyer.

"That's enough!" my mother yelled at them. "I want you both out of this house!" And out the door they went. *Slam!*

That night, all I had were nightmares. I dreamed of the horrible general and the horrible lawyer and how they would have used my magic thinner for horrible things. I dreamed of bringing Bongo back, and then I woke up. I tiptoed over to the window. The rain had stopped and the moon was out. Sailor John was in the courtyard.

He looked up. "Sally, you look sad," he said.

"Bongo's gone," I told him.

"Oh, don't believe that, Sally." And Sailor John started to sing:

In the stillness of my heart I know

It's with you my life I would be sharing,

And if I know you'll be coming home

I would follow deeds of love and daring.

"Sing it with me, Sally," said Sailor John. "You have to know it in your heart."

Suddenly, I understood. I snatched up my father's accordion and started to look wildly around in the pile of thinned items for Bongo. I looked and I looked and finally spotted his tail sticking out from the very bottom. I was so excited I grabbed for it, but his tail tore off in my hand. I let out a gasp, but there was no time to waste. I moved the other items aside and carefully picked up Bongo. I tucked him into the accordion and started to play and sing just like Sailor John:

In the stillness of my heart I know
It's with you my life I would be sharing,
And if I know you'd be coming home
I would follow deeds of love and daring.

Suddenly, a loud bark sprang from the accordion and out dropped Bongo! *"Bow! Wow!"* he barked, as he jumped up on me.

My parents woke up. "Sally!" my father exclaimed. "You remembered how to do it! We'll be rich!"

"I don't remember a thing," I said. "I'm just glad to have everything back the way it should be, especially Bongo. Even without his tail."

⎯⎯⎯

"And that's how the story ends," said Miss Sally, standing up from the bench and smoothing out her skirt. "That's how I saved the world."

"Oh, Grandma, is that story really true?" asked Mary.

"Young lady, everything I tell you is true," said Miss Sally. "Now, let's go and see if that stationmaster has found us a reliable engine."

*I don't remember how this story came about, but I think my fa-
ther would be delighted with it in its final form. Like his own stories, "The Magic Thinner" is a fantasy about something unusual
created out of something common. Put a bunch of household
items in a big washtub and watch out! By the way, the melody I
use, "The Shoals of Herring," is by my brother-in-law, Ewan
MacColl. I just added the lyrics.*

*This story is probably best suited for older kids, but there is a
lesson in here for grown-ups, too. In the rush to make room for so
many things in our compacted lives, it's easy to get frustrated
with the obstacles presented by the real, three-dimensional
world. For example, I live up a long dirt road, and each spring, I
spend a day re-digging the cross ditches that stretch back and
forth across its length. Visitors complain that the ditches make
for a bumpy ride. But without those gullies, the rain would wash
the road away completely. I think that's the lesson Sally learns:
The bumps and obstacles of daily life are as important as anything else. And without them, life would be, well, pretty thin.*

HEAD OF CABBAGE

ONCE UPON A TIME, a boy named Jack planted a vegetable garden. He watered the seedlings, weeded the rows, and added the fertilizer.

One afternoon, Jack accidentally poured too much fertilizer on one of the cabbages. "I hope that won't hurt it," he thought.

At first the cabbage grew to be one foot wide. Then two feet wide. Then five feet wide. Then ten feet wide. And by the end of the summer, it was fifteen feet wide! Jack and his friends had to use a great big lumberjack saw to cut the cabbage free. It was the largest head of cabbage the world had ever seen.

"What are you going to do with such a big cabbage?" asked his friends.

"I think it would be fun to take a trip," said Jack. "Maybe my cabbage will float." And with the help of his friends, he rolled the cabbage out of the garden and—*splash!*—into the nearby river. And believe it or not, the cabbage did float!

"But where will you sit?" asked his friends.

"Right here," said Jack. And he hopped onto the floating cabbage and hollowed out a little cockpit with his penknife.

"But how will you steer?" asked his friends.

"With a sail, of course!" said Jack. And he picked up a big long stick and stuck it into the top of the cabbage to serve as a mast. Then he peeled off one of the biggest cabbage leaves and hoisted it up as a sail.

"But where will you go?" asked his friends.

"Around the world, of course," said Jack. And with a little push, off he went, floating down the river. "So long!" Jack called.

From the river, Jack floated to the bay.

From the bay, he floated to the ocean. Pretty soon, a good wind came along and Jack found himself far out at sea.

He sailed and he sailed. He sailed all the way across to the other side of the Atlantic Ocean, until he bumped into the country of France.

"*Bonjour, mes amis!*" called Jack.

"*Bonjour,* Jack," called the French people. "*Bon voyage!*"

And then Jack sailed down the coast of France, to the country of Spain. *"Buenos días!"* called Jack.

"Buenos días!" called the Spanish people. And Jack went on, greeting everybody he met.

"Gia sou," called Jack to a passing boat of Greek fishermen in the Mediterranean Sea.

"Gia sou," the Greek fishermen called back. "Have you ever thought of sailing through the Suez Canal?"

"No," said Jack. "But if they're willing to take cabbages, I'm willing to go." And the next thing you know, Jack was sailing through the Suez Canal, looking out on the beautiful Egyptian desert. *"Salaam aleicham,"* called Jack.

"Aleicham salaam," called the Egyptian people.

Then he sailed down through the Red Sea, which has a whole chain of mountains on one side, and the next thing you know, he was out in the Indian Ocean, passing Kerala, the spice state of India. For thousands of years people have sailed to Kerala to get pepper and cloves and other kinds of spices. But nobody had ever arrived in a cabbage before. *"Namaskaram,"* called Jack.

"Namaskaram," called the Indian people.

Jack kept on sailing. First, through the Strait of Malacca, between Sumatra and the Malay Peninsula. *"Apa khabar,"* called Jack.

"*Khabar baik*," called the Malaysians. Then Jack sailed up and over to the South China Sea, past Vietnam. "*Xin chào*," called Jack.

"*Xin chào*," called the Vietnamese.

Then past China. "*Ni hao*," called Jack.

"*Ni hao*," called the Chinese.

Then Jack sailed right on over to Japan. "*Konnichiwa*," said Jack.

"*Konnichiwa*, Jack," called the Japanese.

By this time the cabbage was no longer as big as when Jack had started his voyage. You see, whenever he got hungry he would snack on a leaf. Nibble by nibble, Jack was eating up his ship.

So he started across the Pacific Ocean. He went very quickly, perhaps because his ship was getting lighter. He passed Hawaii. "*Aloha*," said Jack.

"*Aloha*," called the Hawaiians.

And as he went through the Panama Canal and into the Caribbean Sea, he saw that all kinds of boats were following him. Big boats and small boats. Jack was famous! "Hello," called Jack.

All the people called back greetings in so many different languages Jack couldn't keep count. And when he reached the Atlantic Ocean, and sailed up to New York City, a great crowd of people welcomed him home. "Hellooooo!" called Jack.

"Hellooooo!" called the Americans.

Of course, Jack's voyage didn't break any records for speed. A cabbage doesn't sail nearly as fast as a regular boat. But all the same, it was the first time anybody had sailed a cabbage around the world, and the city gave Jack a ticker-tape parade.

"Now what will happen to your cabbage?" asked his friends.

"I'll return it to the earth, of course," said Jack. And so Jack sailed his cabbage back through the bay, back up the river, and with everybody's help, rolled it into a great big hole in the compost pile.

After the cabbage had become part of the earth again, Jack put up a little sign:

HERE LIES THE CABBAGE THAT
SAILED AROUND THE WORLD.

For the last story of this section, I leave you with my first. The summer I was eight, I noticed that cabbage heads float quite well in water. At school that year, I made up my first improvised story and told it to my friends. I called it, "Jack and His Head of Cab-bage." It was a ridiculous story. Completely impossible. But the other children did listen. I think the idea of their classmate mak-ing up a story held their attention even more than the story itself.

I can't remember if "Jack and the Beanstalk" served as an in-fluence, but that's possible. I'm sure I was influenced, too, by my father's fantastical stories. And while "Jack" was my earliest at-tempt at story making, it goes without saying I've added things as an adult that I didn't know as a kid: How to say "hello" in so many languages, for instance, or the details about Jack's route of passage. I've even recently found out that Mon petit chou *("my little cabbage") is a term of endearment in French!*

Of course, as with all storytelling, you don't need to take my route. Jack could return to a seaport more familiar to your listeners than New York, such as Chicago by way of the Saint Lawrence Seaway. Just look at a map and choose your own ad-venture. The same goes for languages and countries—maybe your family is Italian or Brazilian or Nigerian. Use whatever de-tails you like and off you go. Bon voyage!

6 Story Beginnings

NOW YOU WANT to make up your own story, but aren't sure where to begin? Not to worry. It's a rare storyteller who isn't stumped at least once in a while.

Musicians borrow old melodies and set new words to them. Why can't storytellers get a similar creative jump start? Here, in the following pages, you'll find a few story beginnings to help you on your way.

Storytellers from William Shakespeare to Woody Guthrie have used this method of taking an old idea to create something new. Not bad company. Go on, give it a try.

GOLDILOCKS

An old classic can make a good first ingredient for any home-made story. When my granddaughter, Moraya, was four or five years old, she loved to hear "Goldilocks." We live in the woods, after all. I must have told her this story for months. I'd try telling her something else and she'd say, "No, tell 'Goldilocks.'" It got so she knew the tale by heart. When Goldilocks came to the door and walked right in without knocking, I'd say, "That wasn't very polite, was it? You should always knock before you go in. Even if the door is open." Moraya had those phrases memorized and she would say them with me.

When telling a familiar story like "Goldilocks," try getting your listener to help with some of the lines like Moraya did. Or try adding your own bear voices—a deep bear voice for Papa Bear, a medium bear voice for Mama Bear, and a squeaky high voice for Baby Bear. Or add your best porridge recipes—maybe one that includes chocolate chips or bananas or honeycomb.

One of the interesting aspects of "Goldilocks" is its flexibility. Take, for instance, its title. It's also known as "Goldilocks and the Three Bears" or simply "The Three Bears." But if you know a family that has two children, you can add an extra member to the bear family. It could be "Goldilocks and the Four Bears." Or perhaps you're a single parent with one child, so you call it "Goldilocks and the Two Bears."

Almost everybody is familiar with this old classic, but we often forget how wide open the ending remains when Goldilocks runs off without saying a word. My version begins with a housing development, but leaves the ending up to you. See what you come up with. Does Goldilocks learn any lessons? Does she return to apologize and fix the chair? Does she become friends with the bears?

THERE WAS ONCE a big, **Big**, **BIG** forest. And near the forest there was a little town. But over the years the town grew and grew, until it came right up to the edge of the forest.

The people didn't give a thought to the animals living there, and the animals weren't happy about this at all. In particular, there was a family of three bears—Papa Bear,

Mama Bear, and Baby Bear—and they said, "If they build many more houses, we're going to have to move."

One day the three bears sat down to supper. Mama Bear had cooked a big pot of porridge and ladled it out into three bowls. But it was still too hot.

Papa Bear said, in a deep bear voice, "Let's take a little walk. We'll come back in a few minutes. By then the porridge will have cooled enough to eat."

"That's a splendid idea," said Mama Bear, in a medium bear voice. When they walked out of the house, they left the door open. After all, they were coming right back.

It so happened that in one of the new houses at the edge of the forest, there lived a little girl named Goldilocks. Her mother had warned her, "Don't go into the woods, Goldilocks. There are *bears* in there."

But what her mother didn't know was that bears made Goldilocks curious. And one day, when her mother wasn't looking . . .

THE SPOT BUG

One role of stories has always been to explain life's little myster-
ies. How did the tiger get its stripes? How did the oak tree get its
acorns? How do kitchen pots get spots? I'm the pot washer in my
family and I've discovered that no matter how much I scrub a
pot, the spots reappear the next day. I realize there are scientific
answers to this question—protein deposits, grease stains, and so
on—but what if it turns out science is mistaken? What if your
home is infested with SPOT BUGS?!

BY DAY, SPOT BUGS live peacefully in kitchen cabinets.
But at night, they get very busy.

Spot bugs roam the dish racks of the world, leaving their
spots where they see fit—pots, pans, glasses. You name it,
the spot bug will spot it.

"Why do people have to take my spots off?" the spot bug asks. Spot bugs consider themselves artists. In the eye of the spot bug, a spot is not simply a spot. Durability must be considered as well as spacing, especially in light of steel wool and harsh cleansers.

This is the story of a spot bug named Spot. He was known throughout the kitchen as the maker of the biggest and most stubborn spots. One night, Spot was at work on his masterpiece, when he thought, "Why do spots always have to be circular?"...

THE MAGIC MOWER

My father was always using ordinary household items in his tales and making them somehow special. This one's about a magic lawn mower. It's just the beginning, but it's an easy story to embellish. What do you think happens?

Just beware! Before you know it, you might have to be logical, and that might be the end of storytelling.

THERE WAS ONCE a newly married couple. The husband was rather forgetful about doing his chores. He needed to be reminded.

"Darling, you must buy a lawn mower," said the man's wife. "The grass is knee-high."

So next morning the man went down to buy himself a new lawn mower at the local hardware supply. This was back in the days when people pushed lawn mowers by hand. Folks didn't have electric or gasoline motors to power their mowers like we do now. You had to push it *hard* to make the spiral blades go round and round. And the longer the grass, the harder it was to push the mower through the grass.

The man brought the new lawn mower home to test it out, but no matter how hard he pushed and shoved and grunted, the lawn mower just wouldn't seem to cut. "This won't do," said the man. "I'll take this mower back to the shop tomorrow." He lay down inside the house and fell sound asleep.

After a while, the man's wife came home. She saw the lawn mower and thought to herself, "Oh wonderful! The new lawn mower. I'll test it out myself."

What she didn't know, was that the mower was a magic mower. . . .

DAVID AND GOLIATH

I mentioned earlier that I like Bible stories because they tend to give the plot, but leave the details up to you. This makes Bible stories excellent for story beginnings—even if you already know the story's ending.

You might explore a part of the story not usually given much attention. For example, prior to his big battle with Goliath, David wasn't just sitting in the mountains reading comic books; he was herding sheep and always practicing with his sling. After all, wolves lived up in those mountains and they like to eat sheep. You might begin telling the story this way. . . .

———

A SLING IS NOTHING but a strip of leather about five feet long, doubled over, with a little pouch in the middle for a stone. You whirl it around and around and around, and then you have to let go of one end at exactly the right moment. If you let go too early, the stone goes into the ground. Let go too late, the stone goes into the sky. But let go at exactly the right instant, the stone finds its mark.

David practiced and practiced with his sling. At first, he could barely hit a bush a few paces away. But year by year he got better and better. Eventually, he could strike down a wolf a hundred yards away.

On the day of the big battle, David woke early. He oiled his sling and selected a few of the smoothest, roundest stones. Well prepared, David set out for the battlefield.

There, at one end of the flat plain strode a giant man with a very long sword. "Where is your champion?" shouted the hulking warrior named Goliath. "I am ready for him."

Was he seven feet tall or eight feet tall? Was he three hundred pounds or four hundred pounds? Certainly Goliath was stronger and fiercer than any man David had ever met. Behind Goliath stood his army, their horses, and all their armor.

Again Goliath called out, "Where is your champion?"

Across the plain stood a huddled mass of mismatched soldiers. From their ranks stepped young David.

Goliath laughed and pointed at the boy. "That's your champion?" he bellowed. "Ha, ha, ha. Ha, ha, ha. Why, he can't even grow a beard yet!"

Goliath's army was laughing, too. "That's their champion! Ha, ha, ha."

And Goliath was still laughing when David readied a perfectly round stone in his sling. . . .

SKY-HIGH SCRAMBLED EGGS

This is another story from my father. Keep in mind that back in the 1920s, airplanes were a new invention. A pilot sat in an open cockpit behind the propeller and engine.

But how did my father end the story? I can't remember. It's up to you.

———

ONCE UPON A TIME there was a very forgetful pilot. He was flying along one day at a comfortable cruising altitude when suddenly he realized he was almost out of gas. He'd forgotten to fill up the fuel tank before taking off. There he was, high in the sky, with no way to get down safely.

But that wasn't the only problem. He'd forgotten to eat his breakfast that morning. "Where can a person find some fuel and something to eat up here?" the pilot asked a passing bird.

The bird squawked and pointed with its wing to a big, puffy cloud. "Funny," thought the pilot, "that cloud looks like a big batch of egg whites ready to be whipped up. Guess I ought to give it a try."

So the pilot flew right into the cloud and the propeller whipped up the egg whites and flipped them back on the engine. The heat of the engine cooked up the eggs and the wind flipped them back to the pilot. "Not bad," said the pilot, and he got all the food he needed.

"Well, that's one problem solved," he thought. He looked around for the bird again. . . .

THE MAPLE TREE

When my kids were young, I told stories about subjects close to home. I often made up stories about trees and birds because we live on a wooded mountainside. I suppose if we had lived in a more urban setting, I might have told stories about pigeons, alley cats, or subway cars.

ONE DAY, a little girl was sitting quietly in the shade of a big maple tree when she heard a voice say, "Oh, you lucky thing. How I wish I could move from place to place like you."

"Who said that?" asked the little girl.

"Me, of course," said the maple tree. And it went right on talking. "I can wave my branches and sway my trunk. I can talk to the wind. I can even talk to the birds. And if you listen very carefully, I can talk to you."

"Yes," said the little girl. "I can hear you. It's wonderful."

"But I can never move from this spot," sighed the tree.

"Really?" said the little girl.

"I'm afraid not," said the tree. "I know when a storm is coming, and the exact times of sunrise and sunset. I even know what's happening in the next valley. But I can't budge."

"If you never move from here, how do you know all these things?"

"The birds that nest in my branches bring me news," said the tree. "And the breezes bring me tiny messages, too, about the weather, the seasons, and even my family."

"You have a family?" asked the little girl.

"Oh, I have a big family. You see that sapling over there? That's one of my children. And that's one over by the driveway. And that's another back there on the hillside."

"Your family sure is spread out," said the little girl.

"Well, if my seeds land too close to me, they won't get enough sunlight. When the wind blows, my seeds spin round and round like little propellers. That way, they land far enough away to grow."

The little girl was fascinated. "You know a lot," she said. "Can I ask you a question?"

"Of course," said the maple tree.

The little girl thought for a moment. . . .

~~The End~~

the BEGINNING

Pete Seeger